AFTA SpringerBriefs in Family Therapy

A publication of the American Family Therapy Academy

Founded in 1977, the **American Family Therapy Academy** is a non-profit organization of leading family therapy teachers, clinicians, program directors, policymakers, researchers, and social scientists dedicated to advancing systemic thinking and practices for families in their social context.

Vision

AFTA envisions a just world by transforming social contexts that promote health, safety, and well-being of all families and communities.

Mission

AFTA's mission is developing, researching, teaching, and disseminating progressive, just family therapy and family-centered practices and policies.

More information about this series at http://www.springer.com/series/11846

Sally St. George · Dan Wulff
Editors

Family Therapy as Socially Transformative Practice

Practical Strategies

AFTA
American Family Therapy Academy

Springer

Editors
Sally St. George
University of Calgary
Calgary, AB
Canada

Dan Wulff
University of Calgary
Calgary, AB
Canada

ISSN 2196-5528 ISSN 2196-5536 (electronic)
AFTA SpringerBriefs in Family Therapy
ISBN 978-3-319-29186-4 ISBN 978-3-319-29188-8 (eBook)
DOI 10.1007/978-3-319-29188-8

Library of Congress Control Number: 2016933320

Printed on acid-free paper

This Springer imprint is published by Springer Nature
The registered company is Springer International Publishing AG Switzerland

Series Editor Foreword

The *AFTA Springer Briefs in Family Therapy* is an official publication of the American Family Therapy Academy. Each volume focuses on the practice and policy implications of innovative systemic research and theory in family therapy and allied fields. Our goal is to make information about families and systemic practices in societal contexts widely accessible in a reader friendly, conversational, and practical style. We have asked the authors to make their personal context, location, and experience visible in their writing. AFTA's core commitment to equality, social responsibility, and justice are represented in each volume.

There is a lot of talk about why social justice is important, but very little to guide practitioners in how to actually talk about it in therapy or put it into practice in our day-to-day work. Sally St. George and Dan Wulff have put together an edited volume that does just that. The authors in *Family Therapy as Socially Transformative Practice: Practical Strategies* provide highly readable personal accounts of how they reveal injustices, help clients work for change, and transform traditional hierarchies and boundaries between knowledge creation and practice, between teacher and learner.

I am especially appreciative that the detail and examples of socially transformative practice in each chapter are jargon-free and easily applicable across theoretical frameworks and clinical models. As the authors note, they do not present a new model or a step-by-step protocol to follow. Instead, they illustrate small actions that can make big changes, changing both the focus of the problem and the locus of change from the individual or family to the wider community and societal discourses and structures. Readers will find themselves considering how they can enact their professional roles through daily practices that confront unfairness, transform hierarchies, and engage communities.

Portland, OR

Carmen Knudson-Martin
Series Editor

Acknowledgments

We wish to gratefully acknowledge Charles Waldegrave and Taimalieutu Kiwi Tamasese from The Family Centre in Wellington, New Zealand, and Cheryl White and David Denborough from the Dulwich Centre in Adelaide, Australia. In their own unique ways they offered us a variety of opportunities to learn and study global and local injustices; they introduced us to practitioners who modeled integrating social justice into one's clinical practice and urged us to experience different contexts to understand the pressures of living in those contexts. Through it all they gave us time to ask questions, feel the pressures, and encouraged us to translate our learnings into our contexts, all while considering our social positions.

Contents

1 **Family Therapy + Social Justice + Daily Practices = Transforming Therapy** 1
Sally St. George and Dan Wulff

2 **Community-Minded Family Therapy** 9
Sally St. George and Dan Wulff

3 **Researcher as Practitioner: Practitioner as Researcher** 25
Dan Wulff and Sally St. George

4 **Supporting the Development of Novice Therapists** 41
Lynda M. Ashbourne, Kelly Fife, Matthew Ridley and Erica Gaylor

5 **Learning to Speak Social Justice Talk in Family Therapy** 57
Lynda J. Snyder, Shannon McIntosh and Faye Gosnell

6 **Everyday Solution-Focused Recursion: When Family Therapy Faculty, Supervisors, Researchers, Students, and Clients Play Well Together** 69
Ron Chenail, Arlene Brett Gordon, Jenna Wilson and Lori Pantaleao

7 **Family Therapy Stories: Stretching Customary Family Therapy Practices** 85
Sally St. George, Dan Wulff, Ron Chenail, Lynda J. Snyder, Lynda M. Ashbourne, Faye Gosnell and Shannon McIntosh

Index 99

Editors and Contributors

About the Editors

Sally St. George Ph.D., RMFT is an Associate Professor and Director of the MSW Clinical Specialization in the Faculty of Social Work at the University of Calgary, and a Family Therapist and Clinical Supervisor at the Calgary Family Therapy Centre. Practicing marriage and family therapy for the last 20 years, she is dedicated to creating and utilizing social constructionist principles in her teaching, research, and clinical practice. Sally is internationally known for her publications and presentations that contain a focus on integrating across micro- and macro-practices as well as across research and clinical/therapeutic practice. In addition, Sally serves on the Boards of Directors for the Taos Institute and Global Partnership for Transformative Social Work both dedicated to living and expanding the practice of social constructionism. She is also the Senior Editor of *The Qualitative Report*, an open-access online interdisciplinary journal which is committed to creating a learning community of writers and reviewers to present solid, interesting, and novel works of qualitative inquiry. Sally's favorite leisure activity is ballroom dancing and her favorite partner is Dan Wulff.

Dan Wulff Ph.D., RMFT, RSW is an Associate Professor in the Faculty of Social Work at the University of Calgary and a Family Therapist and Clinical Supervisor at the Calgary Family Therapy Centre. His research and practice efforts center on an integrative practice of social work and family therapy. Dan also serves on the Boards of Directors for the Taos Institute and Global Partnership for Transformative Social Work as well as serving as a Co-Editor of *The Qualitative Report*.

Contributors

Lynda M. Ashbourne Department of Family Relations and Applied Nutrition (Couple and Family Therapy), University of Guelph, Guelph, ON, Canada

Ron Chenail College of Arts, Humanities, and Social Sciences, Nova Southeastern University, Fort Lauderdale, FL, USA

Kelly Fife Flamborough Women's Resource Centre, Interval House Hamilton, Hamilton, ON, Canada

Erica Gaylor North Simcoe Family Health Team, Midland, ON, Canada

Arlene Brett Gordon College of Arts, Humanities and Social Sciences, Nova Southeastern University, Fort Lauderdale, FL, USA

Faye Gosnell Counselling Psychology, Calgary Family Therapy Centre, Calgary, AB, Canada

Shannon McIntosh Alberta Health Services' Child and Adolescent Addictions and Mental Health, Specialized Services, Calgary, AB, Canada

Lori Pantaleao College of Arts, Humanities and Social Sciences, Nova Southeastern University, Fort Lauderdale, FL, USA

Matthew Ridley Blue Hills Child and Family Centre, Aurora, ON, Canada

Lynda J. Snyder Calgary Family Therapy Centre, Calgary, AB, Canada

Sally St. George Faculty of Social Work, University of Calgary, Calgary, AB, Canada

Jenna Wilson College of Arts, Humanities and Social Sciences, Nova Southeastern University, Fort Lauderdale, FL, USA

Dan Wulff Faculty of Social Work, University of Calgary, Calgary, AB, Canada

Chapter 1
Family Therapy + Social Justice + Daily Practices = Transforming Therapy

Sally St. George and Dan Wulff

Whether we have lived through (or studied the history of) the various generations and approaches to family therapy, we have felt the excitement associated with the dynamism of systemic change, the controversies of turning major accepted ideas upside down, and the experience of shifts in thinking and language. We have followed these changes with great interest and have noted how new and fresh thinking has had a transformative influence in shaping our clinical practices. As family therapists, supervisors, educators, and authors, our goal has been to help transform the field of family therapy by adding a greater focus on the insidious daily ways that unfairnesses/injustices work their way into the lives of our client families and our students as well as our own practices. We do not offer a new approach or model of practice that supplants the systemic grounding upon which family therapy stands—we try to extend our focus onto the larger systemic influences (e.g., societal discourses, structural inequities) that insinuate themselves into the family system, into therapy, into our disciplinary ways of thinking, and into the academy. We hope you will see the connections between our work and the systemic roots that have grounded the field of family therapy throughout its history.

Let us introduce ourselves. As academics in Canada, we are economically privileged and have flexible and secure jobs; we are White; in our 60s; married (to each other); very experienced in teaching, conducting therapy, researching, and supervising in the fields of Marriage and Family Therapy and Social Work; hold identical positions (for the second time in our academic careers) in the Faculty of Social Work at the University of Calgary; and have ample opportunities to voice our ideas with others through teaching and writing. We both hold a view of the world that is grounded in social constructionism (Gergen 2011) and see relationality

S. St. George (✉) · D. Wulff
Faculty of Social Work, University of Calgary, Calgary, AB, Canada
e-mail: sstgeor@ucalgary.ca

D. Wulff
e-mail: calgary_home@shaw.ca

S. St. George and D. Wulff (eds.), *Family Therapy as Socially Transformative Practice*, AFTA SpringerBriefs in Family Therapy,
DOI 10.1007/978-3-319-29188-8_1

as a more generative construct than individualism. This leads us to challenge many received practices of the academy, institutions, and traditions with the intent of creating new pathways toward change.

As social workers and family therapists, we have long attended to the issues of social justice/injustice in our teaching and practices. We have been looking closely at how talk of social justice emerges in family therapy conversations and how therapists respond in those situations. Rarely will the term "social justice" appear in everyday therapeutic discourse, but we have found some proxy language that seems to bring those ideas of unfairness forward. We have been aided in looking for these language practices by Kiwi Tamasese and Charles Waldegrave of the Just Therapy Team (Tamasese et al. 2005; Waldegrave 2009); David Denborough and Cheryl White from the Dulwich Centre (Denborough et al. 2006); and from Canadian colleagues, Vikki Reynolds (Reynolds and Polanco 2012; Reynolds 2013), Alan Wade (Richardson and Wade 2013), and David Paré (Paré 2014).

We were drawn to include the topic of social justice in our clinical work because we saw the increasing pressures that families were experiencing that could not be explained simply by the patterns of their internal family dynamics. Sure, their interactions and solutions at times worsened their situations, but fallout from a steady diet of evaluation, threats, confusions, expectations, blaming, and entitlements emanating from inside *and outside* of the family has helped us to see how families and their members often experience isolation, feelings of unworthiness, lack of success, loss of dreams, and their faltering ability to resist these untenable, unfortunate, and unlivable conditions (see McDowell 2015). Their resistance to the unwanted and life-draining situations of their surround encouraged us to join with them to better understand how these larger conditions and discourses impinge upon their daily lives and to develop ways to limit or alter those conditions.

Therefore, we have modified our listening, our noticing, our languaging, our teaching and supervising, and our researching to try to attend to and include more persons, perspectives, ideas, discourses, and possibilities to help us to more clearly see how these larger structures, discourses, and practices work in the daily troubles that our client families face. We are now recognizing the limitations of understanding families' troubles as originating solely in their interactions with one another. Because we center systems theory, we are constantly reminded of the embeddedness of behaviors within ever-increasing levels of systems—so why have we become so enamored with explaining family difficulties as the exclusive domain of the dynamics within a given family?

Let us provide an example of a family of five who presents for therapy (please note that all identifying information has been modified and the case is presented as a composite to protect confidentiality). The biological mother (white, educated, middle-class, employed as an elementary school teacher) and stepfather (an Indian immigrant, educated, employed in the computer technology business) are exasperated with their 16-year-old daughter who lies, is failing high school, uses marijuana with friends, has been caught having sex in the family home, and has been arrested for stealing. Her parents and other adults (e.g., family friends and teachers) who know her also find this young woman quite lovely, charming, polite, humorous, thoughtful, and protective of her younger stepbrothers who are aged 6 and 8. The parents are equally charming and hardworking, but have developed a stern attitude of discipline using accusation, yelling, and punishment (e.g., withholding of privileges), as well as a stance of "giving up" on their daughter. There is occasional long-distance interaction via Skype with the girl's biological father and his wife who are in the military and stationed overseas.

This problematic interaction includes the daughter and the parents with whom she lives. The therapist proceeded to work with this family by asking them about their backgrounds, their relationships with each other, and the ways in which they problem-solve. In addition, the parents talked about comments made by their employers and coworkers that suggested that "parents coddle their kids too much these days," cannot control them, and then, they need to take them to therapy (and this takes too much time from work). The parents took these statements to mean that *they* were bad parents and their requests for release time from work were pointless and inappropriate. In addition, they also heard innuendos that were critical of blended families and, in particular, mixed racial/cultural families.

The daughter also stated that she "did not care what other people at school say because they don't know what they are talking about anyway." When asked to say more about what she meant, she said that she overheard comments from students and administrators about mixed-race families always being "trouble" and in need of special help and attention. So the difficulties this family were facing were made more problematic because of the climate of comments from around them at work and at school and it is very possible that these community attitudes could themselves create the family's troubles in the first place. Whether these viewpoints created the family's troubles or made the problems they already had worse, the family was dealing with a sense of shame and a need to isolate from the persons who voiced these viewpoints and expectations or who the family believed held these attitudes.

When the team put together all that we heard, we talked about the daily discourses we heard in action: Your family is problematic, you are bad parents, your kids are bad, mixing races and cultures to create a home life is wrong. These discourses had an effect on the family members to feel bad and shamed, and out of this, the family could (a) fight back in a confrontive style that may further ostracize them in the eyes of others, (b) slide into isolation to stay "off the radar" of those who hold these views, or (c) find a way to challenge the limitations posed by these debilitating discourses. These unfair or "unjust" viewpoints are problematic for a number of reasons, most notably because they paint with broad brushstrokes everyone in a group, not acknowledging individual differences. Discriminatory viewpoints are often discussed as "isms" (e.g., racism, sexism, ageism), but in our work, we prefer to approach these discourses of limitation on a more local level, seeing them "at work" in people's lives. These more specific and local manifestations of the big "isms" provide us with access to talk about them and to strategize how to limit or neutralize them, and even to change them.

Holding these discourses in mind, the therapist asked the family if and how these discourses could be related to the family troubles they were experiencing. They saw connections with their experiences, and they began to see how these discourses played out in their lives and others' lives, in big and small ways, and in daily aspects of their lives in many settings (e.g., at school, at work, in the neighborhood, at home, at church). They transferred some of the talk to their workplaces and school by finding ways to question what others were implying and how they were arriving at such conclusions without using open conflict. Inside the family they slowed down to ask the same questions. The problems have not all been solved, but the kinds of conversations have shifted and extended beyond the therapy room. For us, this change in usual practice conversations can help us to question taken-for-granted statements of expectations of normality and acceptability or judgments about intent or what is right and wrong. These embedded assumptions in our social lives are discussed in ways that allow for more critical examination and to connect them with the values/beliefs on which they are based.

We are alerted to the justice issues that families face when we hear talk of feeling "overloaded" (e.g., attempting to give children everything they want, doing work for someone else without acknowledgement or appreciation), pressured into following societal expectations even when sensing it is not what you think you should do (e.g., using tough love, waiting until the bottom falls out), or feeling judged on everything in life (e.g., performances of parenting, being an adolescent, achieving success). We note this talk and inquire about what ideas and messages contribute to these feelings and reactions. We invite our families into a critical examination of these messages for the parts that are useful and the parts that are constraining them from moving in their preferred directions. Such an examination helps us better understand how the problems make sense to the families and what families want to achieve; it also provides avenues that we might explore to increase the family's options for preferred change.

Here is a provisional outline of how we proceed with our families so that we might include talk addressing the justices and injustices in their lives. When families are beginning their therapeutic journey with us and presenting the problems they are experiencing, we often ask:

- What do you find most difficult in this situation?
- *How* is it problematic? (We think it is critical to understand the specific ways a "problem" is "problematic" or troublesome for the family. Given our view that human difficulties are complex, we want to avoid assuming how a situation is problematic for someone else.)

After they have described their difficulties or problematic sequences, we might ask the following questions. These are based in the belief that families are trying to move forward and accomplish something important to them.

- What were you hoping to achieve when the problems or difficulties developed?
- What did you imagine or anticipate when you set out on this path?
- In what ways could it make sense (not that it is desirable) that these difficulties could emerge?

To move forward and to help with the change they most want, we often ask questions about their beliefs, principles for living, and the discourses taken on as their own. The purpose is to come to know what should ground any new actions or solutions we co-construct with them.

- What are the principles (usually they are articulated in the form of discourses, though we do not use that word) that you hold near and dear?
- In what ways have these principles or ideas served you well and in what ways have they fallen short?

Preview of This Volume

We are most fortunate to have colleagues who are also interested in seeing, hearing, and talking social justice issues into our daily therapeutic work with client families and in addressing social justice in academic and supervisory relationships with students. Our commonality seems to be that it is ethical and just to continue to develop our practices to be most effective, inclusive, fair, interesting, and meaningful. And for us that includes examining patterns of clinical practice and supervision through research and inquiry in ways that are congruent within our own daily work. We see valuable connections among clinical practice, supervision, research, and teaching; through all we hold a primary goal of pursuing change, yet all are social practices with the potential to be socially just (or not). It is our collective view that traditional practices in all these arenas would be well served if we regularly re-examined our work as designed and if so how well we attain the goals we envision.

To accomplish this, we have enlisted colleagues who have developed ways to do just this. We will introduce their work to you and highlight some developments in supervision, research, and family therapy practices that are in motion in Canada and the USA. In *Community-Minded Family Therapy,* we (St. George and Wulff 2016) further elaborate our work with societal discourses. We focus on how the discourses "taken up" by families in responding to their difficulties may lead to increasing the blame and shame families feel or perhaps may lead to seeing problems as derivative of contexts and situations outside of families. Locating the problematic discourses/influences outside the family provides the family the opportunity to question expected behaviors with more energy and courage. Examination of these expectations can provide room to consider alternative ways of alleviating their troubles. Traditional mental health practices of helping individuals and families alter their communication and interaction styles remain accessible, but are now supplemented with many ways to address the troubles they face that are located in expectations, "given" roles, and larger group processes that create stress and pain for individuals within the group or community.

In *Researcher as Practitioner: Practitioner as Researcher*, we (St. George and Wulff 2016) introduce our research initiatives based on the principles of what we call "Research As Daily Practice." The focus of this chapter is to reveal how family therapists are in the "perfect" frontline position to conduct "research" and to teach ways to examine the patterns across their caseloads. This local attention to clinical patterns among therapists or across individual therapists' caseloads embraces the idea of critically examining family troubles in terms of how they resemble other families' troubles, increasing the probability of seeing the societal discourses at work in peoples' lives, and creating a common feel among the families that they share issues with others—they are not alone. In Research As Daily Practice, we welcome the involvement of client families in investigating their lives, a process resonant with the social justice initiatives we have been outlining earlier in this chapter.

All new therapists are required to complete studies in diversity. However, the theoretical and the practical may not immediately come together for novices. Lynda Ashbourne, Kelly Fife, Matthew Ridley, and Erica Gaylor (2016) in *Supporting the Development of Novice Therapists* generously provide practical supports in the development of skills in attending to differences between one's own and another's experience and social position. They rely on creating space for dialoguing, using clinical situations to ask supervisees questions that require reflection on the shifting sands of power, and the intersection of the dimensions that comprise one's social location.

Continuing with helping new clinicians incorporate social justice conceptualizing and talk into their new therapy practices, Lynda Snyder, Shannon McIntosh, and Faye Gosnell (2016), in *Learning to Speak Social Justice Talk in Family Therapy*, tell the story of a small research project recounting explicitly the ways in which these skills can be taught and learned. We find out that this is not an easy endeavor as students feel vulnerable in engaging in social justice talk for fear of appearing biased (we also see this occurring in the classroom) and requires avid, courageous, and consistent journeying with supervisors and each other to get the conversations going and to keep them going. They found that it takes explicit and regular attention in the form of reflecting, conversing casually and formally on the part of supervisors and therapists to not let go, especially when the issues touch our own hearts.

Another shift is noticeable from the work of Ron Chenail, Arlene Brett Gordon, Jenna Wilson, and Lori Pantaleao (2016) in *Everyday Solution-Focused Recursion: When Family Therapy Faculty, Supervisors, Researchers, Students, and Clients Play Well Together.* In their campus clinic, they have challenged the "hardening of the categories" across research, practice, and supervision and encourage us to loosen our hold on keeping these family therapy activities separate and rigidly distinct. By embracing and demonstrating a solution-focused, appreciative stance, they have created "playful" and recursive relational patterns that lead to more therapy-informed research, more research-informed clinical practices, and more egalitarian faculty-student relations. The blending they propose, which is built on positive exceptions and hope-filled possibilities, has yielded competent and confident practitioners, teachers, and supervisors who can "walk the theoretical talk" toward change.

Finally, some authors of this volume offer stories of current work and experiences that highlight their newest efforts of enacting the ideas we have presented about transforming therapy based on blending family therapy, social justice, and daily practices. It is our hope that others will be encouraged to share their modifications and additions that can have transformative impact on family therapy practice.

References

Denborough, D., Koolmatrie, C., Mununggirritj, D., Marika, D., Dhurrkay, W., & Yunupingu, M. (2006). Linking stories and initiatives: A narrative approach to working with the skills and knowledge of communities. *The International Journal of Narrative Therapy and Community Work, 2*, 19–51. Available from www.dulwichcentre.com.au

Gergen, K. (2011). *Relational being: Beyond self and community*. New York, NY: Oxford University Press.

McDowell, T. (2015). *Applying critical social theories to family therapy practice (AFTA SpringerBriefs in Family Therapy)*. New York, NY: Springer International. doi:10.1007/978-3-319-15633-0

Paré, D. (2014). Social justice and the word: Keeping diversity alive in therapeutic conversations. *Canadian Journal of Counselling and Psychotherapy, 48*(3), 206–217.

Reynolds, V. (2013). "Leaning in" as imperfect allies in community work. *Narrative and Conflict: Explorations in Theory and Practice, 1*(1), 53–75.

Reynolds, V., & Polanco, M. (2012). An ethical stance for justice-doing in community work and therapy. *Journal of Systemic Therapies, 31*(4), 18–33.

Richardson, C., & Wade, A. (2013). Creating Islands of safety: Contesting failure to protect and mother-blaming in child protection cases of paternal violence against children and mothers. In S. Strega, J. Krane, S. Lapierre, C. Richardson, & R. Carlton (Eds.), *Failure to protect; Moving beyond gendered responses* (pp. 146–186). Winnipeg, Manitoba: Fernwood.

Tamasese, K., Peteru, C., Waldegrave, C., & Bush, A. (2005). Ole Taeao Afua, The new morning: A qualitative investigation into Samoan perspectives on mental health and culturally appropriate services. *Australian and New Zealand Journal of Psychiatry, 39*(4), 300–309.

Waldegrave, C. (2009). Cultural, gender, and socioeconomic contexts in therapeutic and social policy work. *Family Process, 48*(1), 85–101.

Chapter 2
Community-Minded Family Therapy

Sally St. George and Dan Wulff

Introduction

Family therapy often focuses on the intra-family space as the locus of change to help families improve their lives. This may unfortunately convey to the family that the troubles they are facing are caused by what they are doing with one another and therefore it is they, and they alone, who need to make adjustments. We believe that living conditions and societal beliefs within which families live and work contribute in direct and indirect ways to the troubles they experience within their family interactions. When clients find ways to successfully adjust themselves to the conditions and societal discourses of their life worlds, those conditions and discourses remain unexamined as contributors to family troubles and may inadvertently be further re-inscribed as legitimate and "the way it is." In our view, those extra-familial influences should be recognized for the potentially deleterious impacts they may have and in addition, should become our focus to (a) better understand the ways families' lives and decision-making are influenced by the discourses they make their own, and (b) how the discourses might be altered by the families we see in therapy (Waldegrave 2009). Considering this level of mutual influence between families and the larger conditions and scripts they live by is a way of bringing the community (the extra-familial, the societal discourses) into the therapy room, a practice we call *Community-Minded Family Therapy*. By practicing *Community-Minded Family Therapy*, we approach change on two fronts: first, in the service of helping families live more harmoniously and second, launching

S. St. George (✉) · D. Wulff
Faculty of Social Work, University of Calgary, Calgary, AB, Canada
e-mail: sstgeor@ucalgary.ca

D. Wulff
e-mail: calgary_home@shaw.ca

S. St. George and D. Wulff (eds.), *Family Therapy as Socially Transformative Practice*, AFTA SpringerBriefs in Family Therapy,
DOI 10.1007/978-3-319-29188-8_2

initiatives by families and therapists to challenge the contextual factors and discourses that plague us within our communities.

Our Context

We are White, upper middle class, aged 60+ Americans living in an upwardly mobile city in Alberta, Canada, and a married couple working in the same academic setting, the University of Calgary. For the majority of our higher education academic careers, we have directed a marriage and family therapy (MFT) program within a school of social work. We have taught research and practice classes, as well as having our own caseloads of client families. As a result of these diverse activities in two different fields (social work and MFT), we found ourselves feeling quite divided, split, and emotionally harried; we recognized that the discourses surrounding professional specialties created a separateness (as demonstrated in most curricula) that was prominent in the ways that these areas were conceptualized, taught, and practiced. Students and academicians were choosing "camps" of what to believe! While we had heard some encouraging talk of integrating or bridging disciplines, we were not seeing this operationalized and we decided that focusing on "walking the talk" of bridging social work with MFT and research with practice would help us manage all our work. Therefore, we began experimenting with ways in which we could integrate across the curriculum (see Wulff and St. George, Researcher as Practitioner, 2016), our own research programs, and our clinical practices (Wulff and St. George 2014). We constantly asked ourselves, "How is each activity that we are investing in serving our other tasks/goals?" For example, how is the research we are doing and teaching serving practice and vice versa, and especially how can social work and MFT practices come together into an integrated whole? From this desire to connect our work into a coherent whole, we developed *Community-Minded Family Therapy* as a way to bring the extra-familial influences into the focus of therapeutic conversations.

Assumptions Grounding *Community-Minded Family Therapy*

We begin with our guiding assumptions that ground our thinking in this form of practice:

1. Practice decisions and actions impact many other systems beyond the family. Bateson (1972) reminds us of the interconnectedness of all systems (the ripple effect). As members of a common community, the efforts we put forward to change/improve a condition, policy, or practice impact everyone in that community, including us. Therapy is considered to be a part of the community in

which it arises, serving clients *and* the larger community by helping remediate troubles experienced by some. Therapy could be understood as a community initiative to reduce/resolve conflict and to increase harmony (Margolin 1997). This larger macrofunction of therapy is often upstaged by the emphasis on serving the family's wants and needs. Recognition of both functions of therapy broadens our understanding of how therapy works in society, revealing multiple levels of expectations. In *Community-Minded Family Therapy,* there is an overt recognition of how macro- and micro-concerns are inter-related.

2. Persons who directly experience problematic conditions in their daily lives are in the ideal position to understand those conditions and to form actions to change them. Persons a "step away" from the pain or frustration of a problematic situation (e.g., therapists) can offer insights from their perspectives, but the direct frontline experience of a problem is a position like no other. Person(s) who have the most to gain (or lose) rightfully should become the principal actors in what happens.
3. Broad-based understandings derived from multiple stakeholders equip actors with an appreciation of complex understandings that serve to guide designing and executing deliberate actions to alter societal conditions that negatively impact persons in that community/society. Respecting the client's centrality to the trouble, the inclusion of other viewpoints-of-concern can provide a breadth of ideas that clients can benefit from in deciding how to go forward. This broad and inclusionary approach validates the sense of relationality and community that we inhabit, supporting community initiatives in situations that we usually consider to be individual.
4. Family therapists are in a unique position to witness people struggling with dilemmas that are complex and which derive from decisions and practices emanating from systems, people, and ideologies. Therefore, we are obligated to uphold, honor, address, challenge, and extend the complexities by including and working with contradictions, multiplicities, and diversities. Problems that families face are neither simple nor singular so our work with families on change initiatives needs to hold those complexities rather than trying to chop up the ecology (Bateson 1972) by focusing only on parts/fragments, which tends to have the undesirable effect of blaming and pathologizing individuals.

Community-Minded Family Therapy

Community-Minded Family Therapy is not a brand new approach. Throughout the history of family therapy, practitioners have developed therapeutic practices that included extended families, significant others, and other families facing similar troubles (Laqueur 1976; Seikkula and Arnkil 2006; Seikkula and Olson 2003; Speck and Attneave 1973; Speck and Speck 1979; Waldegrave 1990, 2000, 2009). Narrative therapy (Denborough 2008; C. White 2007; M. White 2007) explores the myriad ways that dominant discourses shape peoples' lives, oftentimes leading them into distress without the awareness of the influence of those discourses. *Community-Minded Family Therapy* is a term we use to remind ourselves, and to teach our students, to keep the wider social context of the families we serve in the forefront of our minds. This may involve physically including other persons in the therapy, but short of that, the awareness of systemic interconnectedness of all those persons involved in the lives of our clients should be front-and-center. There are many influences and influencers in the lives of our families who come for therapy and we should be perpetually curious about how they play out in the lives of our families, their difficulties, and their happiness.

One way we do this is by listening for and considering the discourses that we see as part of the daily rules of living or scripts that our clients have "taken up" and taken on as their own ways of living for achieving success. Someone once said, "Fish are the last to understand water," and we imagine the societal discourses or scripts we enact every day to be such a significant part of our daily existence that we do not notice them—they are assumed. Fish exist in a world of water that is necessary for their survival and we humans live within material worlds and discourses that guide our every move to such a degree that we think those aspects of our lives are "givens" or our own ideas. But when we suddenly have trouble breathing, or do not have the musculature to walk, or have our cherished beliefs or values challenged, we have the opportunity to see and experience how life might be with their absence. Societal discourses that we use to tell us what to perceive and how to move in the world are not hard-wired into us—we grow into them gradually and embrace them into the fabric of our lives (C. White 2007; M. White 2007).

As with all assumptions, the more we recognize that our understandings and worlds are shaped in relation to discourses (we literally "see through them"), the more we can embrace the possibilities that are present. When we began seeing the possibilities of the assumptions of *Community-Minded Family Therapy* for family therapy practice, we noticed how oftentimes helpers inadvertently encourage people to adjust to or accept their life conditions and circumstances rather than finding ways to challenge what was stifling them. For example, many practitioners still speak of commonsense solutions, coping, managing, and waiting. Perhaps these words and what they imply can lead to effective actions to improve people's lives, but in most contexts in which families are working hard to come together and live in their preferred ways, these actions could just as easily be referred to "maintaining the status quo"—encouraging people to become satisfied or content with conditions that are not favorable. For example, how many times have we, as therapists, helped people to cope with living in inadequate housing and dangerous living conditions, with trying to budget on insufficient funds to feed a family with healthy foods, or deal silently with discriminations at school or the workplace? How many times have those conversations occurred without a careful reflection on how they may not be in the client's overall or long-term best interest? Can we see that our actions to promote coping might be implicated in actually maintaining the problem or distress? Could we imagine other therapeutic options that not only benefit the families who come to us, but have the potential to challenge those unhealthful conditions or circumstances that hold a role in the troubles for which our client families seek help?

Another factor that has contributed to adding *community-mindedness* to our family therapy practice was watching clients being accused of sabotaging their own success. Frequently, families are trying to address the troubles from the inside only while the problem at least, in part, stems from extra-familial influences. In many of these situations, the families experience failure in changing their lives and this often leads to self-blaming or criticism from others for lacking sufficient will or ability to improve the circumstances of their lives; we think this is an injustice. It is bad enough to misplace accountability for a problem, but to compound that by blaming the person(s) suffering seems particularly cruel.

The following story illustrates how dominant societal discourses (like entitlement, meaning some persons are automatically privileged through birth or being a member of a dominant cultural group, while others are not) intrude into persons' daily lives and decisions. Women in a transitional housing project failed to complete their secondary studies or take their driving tests, but organized and advocated for themselves when the local markets discontinued giving out free holiday food baskets. It appeared to us that in order to understand this in a way that did not blame or view the women as making poor choices and decisions (others before had viewed them this way), we would need to look for an explanation that would open ways to reveal how these behaviors "make sense." One of these alternative understandings could be to look at the social expectations held by people regarding what they are entitled to or could reasonably expect, rather than just focus on the missed opportunities for services or the complaining about something seemingly trivial like free holiday food. If one looked at the discourses-in-motion, the women in this example may have been rallying around their perceived "right" to have holiday food while they were less convinced that they were entitled to education. Conceptualizing families in pain as solely responsible for their own trouble flows out of a belief that we are all free-standing individuals who make our own ways in life. This individualistic perspective fuels accountability and responsibility, but it also shields us from understanding how influential others and other ideas are in our lives (Wulff et al. 2011).

We are not only talking about serving those deemed poor and/or disenfranchised. Our goal was to bring attention to societal discourses within our therapeutic work (Chenfeng and Galick 2015) with all families as well as attending to the levels of solutions or locations of emphasis and potential that we create and develop with our families. Introducing the idea of societal discourses as implicated in the lives of families in trouble requires a careful practical presentation of the use of everyday language to link societal discourses with trouble. Examining societal discourses is not just an intellectual argument; we believe there are ways to discuss these influences that anyone could appreciate.

We begin with families by explaining what we see discourses to be and how we see them as influential and implicated in family troubles. For example, if we detect a discourse that tends to valorize defending traditional practices (e.g., "this is the way our families have always done this," "we need to stay true to the ways we learned," "I learned this way and I am okay"), we might ask, "Is this way of relating something that you have seen before in other families or in your families-of-origin?" Or if we hear talk of wanting to do things in order to be accepted (e.g., "all the cool kids have phones," "I will be the laughing stock if I can't go," "I really do not want to have the other parents in the car pool to know we have this trouble") as an overarching theme, we could ask, "How does the trouble you describe show your desire to belong and to be accepted?" (Questions adapted from St. George et al. 2015b). We acknowledge that including this talk in therapy sessions may appear a bit unconventional as compared to traditional psychotherapy, but based upon our supporting premises, we are looking for ways to raise alternative explanations about the troubles families face. To do this may require stepping out of customary therapeutic conversation and questions and into new conversations that specifically discuss the larger systems and discourses.

Considering that client families in trouble are experiencing difficulties that other families not in therapy could more readily understand suggests that external forces/pressures are pervasive in our social worlds. This raises the possibility that families might very productively join together in therapy (or outside of therapy) with other families. Their collective understanding of their lives and their experiences may add new ideas to their ways of going forward. Our point here is that keeping families apart in their own individual therapy sessions when they have a great deal in common with each other may be limiting the progress that could be made; if we made it possible for these families to connect in joint therapeutic sessions (while still honoring families' preferences for confidentiality/privacy and individual family therapy if they wished), we would open new avenues for therapy to make a difference.

Another point we would like to emphasize is that trying to produce change at a family level only without examining how community or societal levels are involved in the family's trouble is not only likely to be ineffective, it is unfair and socially unjust (Almeida 2013; Parker and McDowell, in press; Richardson and Wade 2013; Waldegrave 2009). Repeating an earlier message, it seems to place blame or responsibility (perhaps inadvertently) on the family as if they were the source of the problem and its continuance. Alternatively, if we can examine those societal ideas that they have taken on as their rules for living and as their measures for success, we can develop a variety of possibilities for new conversations and paths toward change inside and outside of families that fit with a contextual understanding of the troubles that the family is experiencing. The larger systems and discourses now go under the therapeutic gaze.

We would also like to emphasize that *Community-Minded Family Therapy* is bi-directional, that is, not only do we assist families in their efforts to improve their lives, but we also bring the community into therapy by examining how the societal discourses work their way into family behaviors and by inviting others into therapy as supportive partners to the family. The potential exists that what happens in therapy can ripple out into the community by the involvement of significant others as well as by how family members take the learnings they develop through therapy into their "other" lives as students, employees, neighbors, or community members.

The boundary between "inside" therapy and "outside" therapy becomes more permeable—therapy becomes more overtly integrated and available within the community. This may lessen the stigma associated with therapy that may come from the secrecy surrounding it.

Bringing the Community into Therapy

What has been done. Others have written about expanding the therapeutic system by inviting "outsiders" to therapy (Denborough 2008; Dulwich Centre 1999; Seikkula and Arnkil 2006; Wulff 1994). These practitioners have included extended family members, or used reflecting teams and witnessing practices, or brought in supportive networks either in person or by distance communications. Often families are reticent to bring in others because they see their problems as private and feel a sense of shame should others know of their distress. When using one-way mirrors, we demystify the situation by having observers or reflectors (often our supervisees) come into the room with the family to share their immediate reactions, ideas, solutions, doubts, and what they are noticing. When we see families' problems as common to those that many families experience, other families and not just professionals can be effectively used as reflectors or contributors to assist fellow families respond to troubling life circumstances. This expansion of the therapeutic system encourages clients to reach out to others rather than becoming isolative in their distress (Wulff and St. George 2011).

Calling upon former clients. Another way of bringing the community into therapy is by asking families who have "graduated" from therapy to join us to offer support and stories of change (White 2007a, b). The inclusion of outsiders is not unlike what happens in group therapy except the conversations are between two families (rather than groups of individuals) as they recount their experiences, worries, fears, and hopes and listen to the others. We ask families as they are getting ready to end therapy if they would be interested in being called upon to help other families with similar dilemmas by joining in the conversation as a "consultant." Many say yes because they would like to be of help to others and they feel validated by being invited to share their wisdom. If current families are amenable to expanding the system in this way, we bring the families together in the same room. They are interviewed together: we ask for their theories of the difficulties they face or have faced, we ask about the typical kind of advice they are given or have been given, we ask about small successes and glimmers of light, we ask about preferred futures, and we ask about being helped and being helpers at the same time. As you can see, the particulars about the troubled families' lives that bring them to therapy are usually not the centerpiece of these meetings, though they may be revealed in the course of the conversation. Primarily we are looking for the conversation to focus on ways to go forward by using the commonalities between families and their experiences very similar to Almeida's work (Almeida and Durkin 1999) through the Cultural Context Model.

We have written elsewhere about the possible unfortunate consequences of confidentiality policies and practices that create a sense of isolation around families which can prevent support from being offered and accepted (Wulff et al. 2011). While we are not advocating for the dismissal of confidentiality practices, we are taking a close look at the ways in which confidentiality and privacy cloister people in their pain seriously hindering their abilities to move on successfully. Confidentiality is a therapeutic practice that is typically unreflectively applied and deserves close scrutiny for its tendency to influence therapists to keep clients apart, and in a sense, encouraging isolation. Ironically, isolation may be the primary culprit in keeping clients from being able to move forward into new and improved patterns of interacting.

Collegial meetings to generate new ideas. Many of our workplaces are currently experiencing shortages in terms of funding, personnel, supervision, time for reflection, and peer consultation and support. “Accountability” practices have stressed fidelity to certain protocols/models and a concentration on reaching pre-set target goals for clients which often leave practitioners feeling tired, constrained, and pessimistic about producing viable and sustainable change with their clients. To counter this increasingly rapid closure of creative space, we have initiated bi-monthly meetings held in our home on Saturday mornings inviting practitioners across the helping professions, from all levels of expertise and types of service providers. We made the focus of these meetings talk about infusing social justice into our therapeutic work. We operate at two levels here. The first is learning how to listen for justice talk that our clients might offer, ways in which we take, decline, or miss the invitation along with instances in which our workplace contexts are implicated in injustices, and secondly, proposing smaller changes we might introduce. We have coffee and conversation; the conversation is generated by questions or stories that one participant may bring forward, usually coming from a recent experience or reflection on something observed. The value of these meetings is evidenced by the attendance—on the weekend, after hours, and unpaid. To use one’s time to do this is a testimony to the importance of these gatherings.

For example, a recent Saturday morning meeting conversation centered on agency meetings when typically all service providers come together to discuss a client’s progress and future plans. As we complained about the usual disciplinary hierarchies that are evident in these meetings and the type of languaging used, we imagined what it might be like if questions were posed to the group as a whole rather than focusing on individual therapeutic reports from individual practitioners (e.g., a psychologist’s report on testing, a physician’s report on medical conditions, a psychiatrist’s report on psychological makeup, a social worker’s report on community supports and services). While these are useful aspects to discuss, they are effectively mentioned in written reports—conjoint professional meetings could attend to the relationships between the workers and the family. Some of the alternative questions we generated included,

1. What ideas have been stimulated in you after reading the various professional reports about this client?

2. Is this client moving in a hopeful direction? Are we contributing to this success? If so, how (specifically)? If not, what are we doing that inhibits progress?
3. What questions linger or what new questions have emerged that you would like to discuss with the other professionals working with this client/family?
4. Which of our efforts hold the most promise in the short term? Which have the greatest chance to be durable/sustainable?

Another example that the group discussed has to do with the situation in which a client is making progress but not fast enough in the allotted time frame. This usually results in a discontinuation of services temporarily and then a new start-up in the agency or in another agency. In addition to lobbying for the client to continue needed services, the therapist could see this as an opportunity to research more thoroughly how services failed to reach the desired goal. This could be done by contacting other professionals and other agencies to see if this problem has some pattern to it (e.g., occurs with certain types of clients, at certain times of the year, in conjunction with some types of services) (St. George et al. 2015a; Wulff and St. George 2014). This project would look at a myriad of factors that could have been involved in the service failure—including systemic issues within the agency or the helping network as well as client factors. This illustrates how "failed" work with clients could launch efforts to more closely examine our practices and potentially improve them.

Working transdisciplinarily. Our first attempt at working transdisciplinarily occurred at the University of Louisville where our students were graduating with a Master's degree in social work *and* a credential in MFT (see Wulff and St. George, Researcher as Practitioner: Practitioner as Researcher, 2016). We worked to create transdisciplinary professionals who would conceptualize their work with families through their chosen "micro-" approaches while simultaneously factoring in the larger context and social justice overlay they studied in their social work courses. We worked hard to have their program become a practical demonstration of how two helping disciplines can be strengthened through mutual influence. To accomplish this, we would constantly ask:

- "What are all the ways we can imagine how this family's problems and unsatisfying dynamics make sense?"
- "Throughout everything, what is this family working to try to accomplish?"
- "What are the invisible forces blocking their movement toward what they are trying to accomplish?"

When the accrediting bodies from both social work and MFT came to interview our students, each group asked our students whether they saw themselves as social workers *or* MFTs. They answered: "We see that question as asking us to choose one set of skills over another, not appreciating how we have blended them into a set of practices that enhance both sets. We cannot *not* see the larger context of the family's dynamics and the multiplicity of forces (macro and micro) that impact the troubles our client families face." We think the idea of merging disciplines in the helping fields is a viable and important path to pursue. Our professional tendencies to specialize into discrete activities that are not integrated or only loosely interconnected pose significant problems for clients who must manage the integration for these multiple services—they must create the sense of coherence of all these helping initiatives.

"As if." One more way of bringing the community into therapy is through "as if" thinking and exercises (Anderson 1997; St. George 1996). "As if" thinking usually involves supervision or large group consultation regarding a therapeutic situation. A therapist presents a case situation to a listening group who has been divided into various listening positions to correspond with the different actors in the case situation (e.g., client, relative, spouse, co-worker, therapist, neighbor, teacher). In a given situation, one of the *as if* listeners might listen to the consultation conversation from the position of an exhausted mother, or a 13-year-old blind daughter, or a stepson who is engaging in reckless behaviors. Rather than listening from one's home disciplinary position, each *as if* listener listens from a different specific position in the case situation, trying to fit into those "shoes" rather than from a professional posture.

When the story has been told, the therapist and supervisor listen to the reactions of the *as if* participants as they express what thoughts they had about the situation of interest, what they thought was perhaps a misunderstanding, or what could be thought about but not asked about. They offer some fresh unrehearsed and unscripted ideas for the therapist and supervisor to take into consideration for future conversations regarding this case. Of course, the *as if* reactions do not represent the "truth," but they allow for much that is possible yet unspoken, to be spoken—a way of transforming one's work and including social justice issues.

Creating and using teams. We like the idea and experience of using teams. However, this can be an expensive and time-consuming proposition. Therefore, we have developed an alternative if we cannot gather a team in the same room. The idea is based on the notion that we are all made up of multiple selves and hold many different ideas about those selves. We bring together the "multiple selves team" without cost or extra time. We have only begun this kind of thinking and are trying it with our students: We ask them to provide explanations of what is happening with a given client or client situation from their "inner" geographer, public policy analyst, accountant, manager, therapist, public citizen, investor, neighbor, dietician, medical provider, or educator. We have them role play sessions making observations and suggestions from these different *as if* positions. It works well when any of us find ourselves stuck with a family's situation and need to find a way to think from some new vantage points. This is a good exercise to stretch our thinking and help us to avoid narrowing our approaches to families that can come from influential disciplinary training or repetitive professional experiences.

Bringing Therapy into the Community

We have some lovely examples from some international colleagues of moving therapy into the community that we have adapted to our context.

The Just Therapy Team. The Just Therapy Team from New Zealand has been an inspiration for us. The Just Therapy Team looks for patterns across their client families similar to our Research As Daily Practice strategy (St. George et al. 2015a; Wulff and St. George 2014). For example, they might notice that an increase in domestic violence is not solely part of an intra-family dynamic; that across these families there were common denominators such as job loss or insufficient housing. Their strategy for change is to work on multiple levels, including going to the community or government for assistance or modifications of policies. If there are not receptive ears at that level, they would consider going to the media to reach the public in order to reveal the conditions that are oppressing families in their communities. The point is not to expose their clients to scrutiny but rather the conditions of their lives that are implicated in their distress. The situations and circumstances revealed in the family's distress are the focus; the distress points us toward the conditions of concern that need addressing. It is similar to the "canary in the coal mine" idea—the toxic conditions in the coal mine are noticed and revealed through the canary's sensitivity to those conditions. The canaries (and our troubled families) serve as an early-warning system that something is amiss. To treat the canary (or the family) without addressing the conditions that led to the distress is doomed to failure, the canary (and the family) will simply be re-traumatized by those persistent conditions. This idea is a significant turn from seeing the client family as the locus of the trouble and the persons who need to change. Our attention is directed to work for change in the *conditions* that led to the families' suffering, not only the sufferers of those conditions—they deserve support but the toxic conditions need the reformation.

We all could do that, too, by studying the patterns across our client caseloads. We have done similar things in our own ways—not by going to the media, but by presenting findings from our Research As Daily Practice to other professionals, students, parent groups, and corporations. An illustration is that we have found that adolescents, especially those from financially stable families, may seem lazy, rebellious, apathetic, or selfish. However, upon a closer look we were able to see these adolescents from another vantage point. We noticed another common pattern—they were tired of (and distrustful of) being evaluated (positively *and* negatively) and were withdrawing from the constant pressure of being scrutinized by others, especially the adults in their lives. These messages about being evaluated alerted us to the many ways in which evaluative talk is frequently used in our therapy sessions and we actively wondered about how evaluative language was used in our questions about intended meanings, unintended consequences, accuracies and inaccuracies of the messages, and examination for what was desired.

By looking for the larger patterns in the lives of our client families, we can see how parents and children living together includes bringing in certain practices and patterns that we adopt from our peers and neighbors and how bringing these all together in our family living may increase the difficulties we have with one another. Looking for the sense that our interactions make allows us to stay in contact with each other and to wonder about how our intentions with one another can be understood. These efforts are strikingly different from approaches that focus on pathological behaviors and intentions.

Community Therapy. We have learned about a second very impressive example of taking therapy to the community from our Brazilian colleague, Marilene Grandesso. She and her colleagues literally bring together community members to serve as helpers to one another. They do this in a community setting of any number of people, often hundreds and thousands at a time. They describe their work as responding "to various forms of social suffering and 'psychic misery'" (Barreto and Grandesso 2010, p. 33) by honoring the people's local knowledge alongside professional knowledge. Using a stage-like process in this large community meeting, small groups of people discuss the issue brought forward by sharing how they, too, are affected by the problem up for discussion (e.g., discriminations, isolation, fears) and ways to alleviate the problem. They describe this as a "shared space of suffering…a process of offering and sharing strategies of dealing with suffering…a public space approach which enable participants to become the doctors of their own experience" (p. 37).

We love this idea, but, in North America where privacy prevails, this becomes a challenging proposition. Perhaps we could do this on a smaller scale or by tailoring other ways of bringing the community into therapy. For example, maybe we could bring back some of the ideas of multiple family therapy, especially when we see our families suffering in similar ways. Instead of seeing one family in therapy, we could see several in one session (Wulff 1994). We could use mirrors or just have cross-family conversations, much the way that some of the domestic violence programs have multiple couples groups (Stith et al. 2011). To proceed down this path, we would emphasize building skills of group facilitation and diminish behaviors that uphold expert authority. These practices could drastically alter how we see therapy today.

Conversations about discourses. When we use the idea of discourses in therapeutic conversations (without specifically calling them "discourses"), we have found that our clients have routinely taken them beyond the therapy room and even outside of their families. We are often finding that talk about unfairnesses such as certain people in the family and the workplace having voice or taking up shared space disproportionately has filtered into their workplaces, circles of friends, and schools. They are becoming quiet activists for changing language and practices in their communities. To illustrate, in a therapy session, parents talked about the use, and effects, of "smart remarks" and sarcasm for "teaching" their children and began to see the connection of those behaviors to language practices in the media (e.g., television sitcoms, popular music, cartoons, and videogames). They became uncomfortable as they saw those behaviors as hurtful and not at all what they intended. This issue was no longer "funny"; they sensed that they had been duped into thinking that these smart remarks were harmless and perhaps even desirable. They also realized that everyone in their family was using this language convention with each other and even in their relationships outside of the home. Without fanfare or telling anyone else, they began to change their own language with their peers and noticed how their change could impact their relationships at school and work.

They were pleased with the development of more appreciative interactions and an understanding of how they could be influential in their relationships.

Working transdisciplinarily. We are advocates for taking therapy into the community in small daily ways—no initiatives, money, or strategic planning is necessary. We favor recruiting our fellow professionals into a different kind of talk, joining with community groups (Doherty et al. 2010). We often talk with groups in large corporations, small teams of cross-disciplinary therapists, staff who work at residential treatment centers, parent groups, and researchers who are planning qualitative inquiries. Our process follows the pattern of examining the language that is being used, the hopes people have for using such languaging, the success rate of accomplishing the hoped-for results, the effects of using that languaging, and then helping to refine the language to help achieve greater success. For example, a single, unemployed mother of eight children who was struggling with serious behavioral issues of some of her children, grinding poverty, and racial discord in her neighborhood was receiving social and mental health services that were organized around the goal of helping her become independent from services. Examining the multiple stressors in her life seemed to render the goal of helping her achieve independence a bit far-fetched. Another perspective might have approached this client from a position of locating ways to support her in coordinated and effective ways now and in the future. Using these alternative approaches challenges the preferred institutional patterns that oftentimes are designed mainly to benefit the institution. To coax an institution into seriously examining alternatives would require a presentation that demonstrates how the agency or institution would benefit by a new approach (this may be no small task).

A great deal of this alternative work is conducted outside of the bounds of regular service providers (e.g., established and funded agencies and programs). For example, we created a "public" practice on a pro bono basis inviting agency practitioners to allow us to work with those families who have seemed to exhaust or have become exhausted by the system. In our current setting, we are planning to pilot an "Impossible" Cases Clinic staffed by interdisciplinary teams of students and professional supervisors to act as consultants to pervasive and non-changing situations. The challenge posed by so-called impossible or intractable cases points toward the helping system to re-evaluate its approach, rather than criticize or demonize the client that it does not seem to be able to help (Duncan et al. 1997).

We have found that "opening up" therapy in the ways we have outlined in this chapter raises interesting questions about the designation and role of "expert." Professional helpers have training in certain areas of understanding but without abiding connections within their community, professionals can become isolated (just as clients can) and miss out on the possibilities of collaboration. When communities of people (of all backgrounds) work together on projects, important actions can occur. We know this from experiences of seeing persons facing calamitous situations who are helped immediately and profoundly by their neighbors. Traditional therapy is also amenable to such processes and can be a part of a collective of resources of both professional and non-professional natures. Rather than hide distress and make it a private affair, perhaps we need to think more seriously about the healing powers of communities and enlist them when families struggle.

Conclusion

Therapy is an activity that occurs within communities. It helps members of those communities to manage stress and trouble in their lives. It is not separated from communities—it becomes a service that occurs within communities. Seeing therapy as apart from communities and indeed a private affair misses the intimate connection that exists. Persons who go to therapy are seeking to live more successfully within their communities and communities are hoping that therapy works.

The relationship only begins there in our view. The possibilities of communities to support therapy and for therapy to influence community life are rich and varied. In this chapter, we have tried to direct our professional viewpoints toward greater acknowledgement of our role in community living and some potential avenues for more explicit connection.

References

Almeida, R. (2013). Cultural equity and the displacement of othering. In *Encyclopedia of social work*. Oxford University Press. doi:10.1093/acrefore/9780199975839.013.889

Almeida, R., & Durkin, T. (1999). The cultural context model: Therapy for couples with domestic violence. *Journal of Marital and Family Therapy, 25*(3), 313–324.

Anderson, H. (1997). *Conversation, language, and possibilities: A postmodern approach to therapy*. New York, NY: Basic Books.

Barreto, A., & Grandesso, M. (2010). Community therapy: A participatory response to psychic misery. *The International Journal of Narrative Therapy and Community Work, 4*, 33–41.

Bateson, G. (1972). *Steps to an ecology of mind*. New York, NY: Ballantine.

Chenfeng, J. L., & Galick, A. (2015). How gender discourses hijack couple therapy—And how to avoid it. In C. Knudson-Martin, M. A. Wells, & S. K. Samman (Eds.), *Socio-emotional relationship therapy: Bridging emotion, societal context, and couple interaction* (AFTA SpringerBriefs in Family Therapy, pp. 41–52). New York, NY: Springer International. doi:10.1007/978-3-319-13398-0

Denborough, D. (2008). *Collective narrative practice: Responding to individuals, groups, and communities who have experienced trauma*. Adelaide, South Australia: Dulwich Centre.

Doherty, W. J., Mendenhall, T. J., & Berge, J. M. (2010). The families and democracy and citizen health care project. *Journal of Marital and Family Therapy, 36*(4), 389–402.

Dulwich Centre. (1999). *Extending narrative therapy: A collection of practice-based papers*. Adelaide, South Australia: Dulwich Centre.

Duncan, B. L., Hubble, M. A., & Miller, S. D. (1997). *Psychotherapy with "Impossible" cases: The efficient treatment of therapy veterans*. New York, NY: W. W. Norton.

Laqueur, H. P. (1976). Multiple family therapy. In P. J. Guerin Jr (Ed.), *Family therapy: Theory and practice* (pp. 405–416). New York, NY: Gardner Press.

Margolin, L. (1997). *Under the cover of kindness: The invention of social work.* Charlottesville, VA: University of Virginia Press.
Richardson, C., & Wade, A. (2013). Creating Islands of safety: Contesting failure to protect and mother-blaming in child protection cases of paternal violence against children and mothers. In S. Strega, J. Krane, S. Lapierre, C. Richardson, & R. Carlton (Eds.), *Failure to protect: Moving beyond gendered responses* (pp. 146–186). Winnipeg, Manitoba: Fernwood.
Seikkula, J., & Arnkil, T. E. (2006). *Dialogical meetings in social networks.* New York, NY: Karnac.
Seikkula, J., & Olson, M. E. (2003). The open dialogue approach to acute psychosis: Its poetics and micropolitics. *Family Process, 42*(3), 403–418.
Speck, R. V., & Attneave, C. L. (1973). *Family networks: A way toward retribalization and healing in family crises.* New York, NY: Pantheon Books.
Speck, R. V., & Speck, J. L. (1979). On networks: Network therapy, network intervention and networking. *International Journal of Family Therapy, 1*(4), 333–337.
St. George, S. (1996). Using "as if" processes in family therapy supervision. *The Family Journal: Counseling and Therapy for Couples and Families, 4*, 357–365.
St. George, S., Wulff, D., & Tomm, K. (2015a). Research as daily practice. *Journal of Systemic Therapies, 34*(2), 3–14.
St. George, S., Wulff, D., & Tomm, K. (2015b). Talking societal discourse into family therapy: A situational analysis of the relationships between societal expectations and parent-child conflict. *Journal of Systemic Therapies, 34*(2), 15–30.
Stith, S. M., McCollum, E. E., & Rosen, K. H. (2011). *Couples therapy for domestic violence: Finding safe solutions.* Washington, DC: American Psychological Association.
Waldegrave, C. (1990). Social justice and family therapy. *Dulwich Centre Newsletter, 1*, 5–47.
Waldegrave, C. (2000). "Just Therapy" with families and communities. In G. Burford & J. Hudson (Eds.), *Family group conferencing: New directions in community-centred child and family practice* (pp. 153–163). New York, NY: Aldine deGruyter.
Waldegrave, C. (2009). Cultural, gender, and socioeconomic contexts in therapeutic and social policy work. *Family Process, 48*(1), 85–101.
White, C. (Ed.). (2007). Experience consultants (entire issue). *The International Journal of Narrative Therapy and Community Work, 27*(2).
White, M. (2007). *Maps of narrative practice.* New York, NY: W. W. Norton.
Wulff, D. (1994). *Families on both sides of the mirror: A structural variation of the multiple family therapy model (Unpublished doctoral dissertation).* Ames, IA: Iowa State University.
Wulff, D., & St. George, S. (2011). Family therapy with a larger aim. In S. Witkin (Ed.), *Social construction and social work practice: Interpretations and innovations* (pp. 211–239). New York, NY: Columbia University Press.
Wulff, D., & St. George, S. (2014). Research as daily practice. In G. Simon & A. Chard (Eds.), *Systemic inquiry: Innovations in reflexive practice research* (pp. 292–308). London, UK: Everything is Connected Press.
Wulff, D., St. George, S., & Besthorn, F. (2011). Revisiting confidentiality: Observations from family therapy practice. *Journal of Family Therapy, 33*, 199–214. doi:10.1111/j.1467-6427.2010.00514.x

Chapter 3
Researcher as Practitioner: Practitioner as Researcher

Dan Wulff and Sally St. George

Researcher as Practitioner: Practitioner as Researcher

We have spent a fair bit of our time as academics and practitioners trying to reconcile the divide between research and practice. Over time, we have even worked in ways that do not distinguish these endeavors from one another in the first place. By overlaying or mapping each onto the other (Wulff and St. George 2014), the differences have been reduced to vocabulary and traditional disciplinary practices. Envisioning research as separate from practice largely sections off the process of inquiry from clinical practice. Inquiry becomes its own field, separate from applying knowledge to help transform our worlds. By replacing inquiry into practice, clinical work can access systematic ways of knowing once again, allowing us to see patterns in our work with client families. Practice-based evidence brings the clinical practice world into a more holistic system of knowing that serves to enhance the therapeutic possibilities for clients we see.

In this chapter, we will describe three ways in which we have worked to close the gap between research and practice in the graduate classroom. First, we will present how we have taught an integrated research and practice course in a joint social work/marriage and family therapy (MFT) program; second, we will discuss how we currently teach Research As Daily Practice early in a graduate-level research class in a social work program; and third, we will showcase how we teach practitioners to be effective consumers of research by using their clinical questioning skills and problem-based learning to appraise research articles and projects. Each of these projects in their own way presented the ideas we commonly consider

D. Wulff (✉) · S. St. George
University of Calgary, Calgary, AB, Canada
e-mail: calgary_home@shaw.ca

S. St. George
e-mail: sstgeor@ucalgary.ca

S. St. George and D. Wulff (eds.), *Family Therapy as Socially Transformative Practice*, AFTA SpringerBriefs in Family Therapy,
DOI 10.1007/978-3-319-29188-8_3

to be associated with research as close kin with ideas we commonly consider to be associated with practice (see Everyday Solution-Focused Recursion: When Family Therapy Faculty, Supervisors, Researchers, Students, and Clients Play Well Together, Chenail, Brett Gordon, Wilson and Pantaleao, 2016). Outcomes from these projects have been most gratifying and have served to stimulate new ways to push forward the idea that research and practice are close siblings, if not twins.

Integrating

In our academic and practice careers we have worked to integrate our various assignments (e.g., teaching, practicing, researching) in order to be efficient and in so doing, we have come to realize that the intersections between these activities are a fertile zone of creativity and generativity. We have found the blending of social work and family therapy to stretch both disciplines in ways that increase the possibilities for effective work with clients. Merging micropractice (face-to-face interaction skills) and macropractice (appreciation of larger systemic influences on persons) similarly allows for a broader and more nuanced understanding of peoples' lives. In this chapter, we will discuss how we have worked the borders between research and practice to see how they can support and enhance one another in fundamental ways for the benefit of clients and the development of new insights. Shaw and Lunt (2012) have expressed it this way:

> We doubt whether it is helpful to envisage practitioner research as being either inside or outside practice or research. The understanding that seems best to depict the experience of our practitioner participants is to see them, in their practitioner-as-researcher work, as outside, or at least on the margins of both research *and* practice—an uncomfortable but creative marginalization. (p. 207)

Imagine a Venn diagram of two intersecting circles with a limited margin of intersection—that is the site of creative and generative conceptualizing and associated practices. This is the zone where practice and research are not readily distinguishable (Fig. 3.1).

We could consider ourselves *on the edge* of each endeavor (practice and research) as well as *in* the intersection of the two. This positioning in the worlds of both practice and research has been an effective form of presenting these ideas to our students.

Fig. 3.1 The zone where practice and research are not readily distinguishable

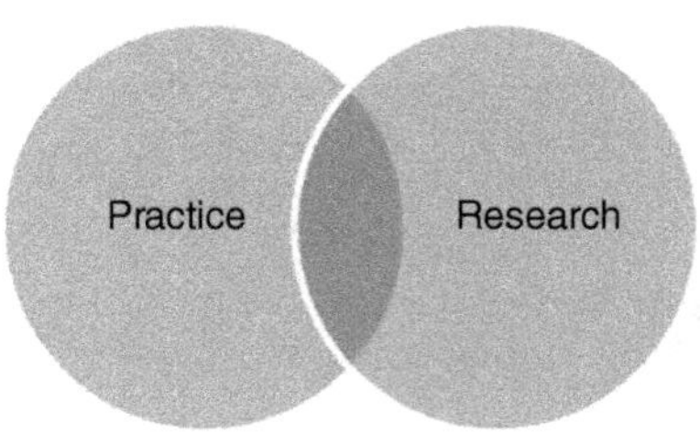

Research as Intervention

Originally, our intentions at working to close the gap between practice and research were to respond to student complaints that research has no practical relevance in clinical practice, that it was difficult to understand, and that clinicians would certainly not be conducting research themselves. We began by recognizing the accuracy of what they were saying from their points of view and experiences. They experienced research as expendable for their practices, it was written in language conventions that were narrow and specific to scientific audiences, and they saw no need to do research in their role as a practitioner. To stimulate our thinking, we examined each of these points and worked from contrary assumptions that,

- Research *was* fundamental and necessary to good practice,
- Research *could be* effectively written in everyday language, and
- Research was something that practitioners could easily do within their practices (and probably *already were doing*).

Working from these premises, we imagined how thinking in these ways could guide our own teaching and supervising of student clinicians, as well as our own practices and research projects.

New ways of teaching and demonstrating practice and research also evolved, requiring time and opportunity to try out these ideas—but no extra money was needed. In a time when research is increasingly dependent upon external funding (and all that comes with such dependence), these ideas could be implemented within existing practice and research structures and the outcomes and benefits were immediate.

We also want to underscore the importance of integrating research and practice with the express purpose of producing change in peoples' lives. This is not an academic exercise—we hope to fundamentally alter our approaches to research and practice in ways that sharpen our attention to social conditions and practices that inhibit individuals, families, and communities.

The Researching Practitioner

In the Kent School of Social Work at the University of Louisville, we wanted to develop a new course design that would allow the graduate students in our integrated social work and family therapy program to experiment with a variety of ways that practice and research could be seen as connected. We created a course that we called "The Researching Practitioner" merging all the content in the practice class that was customarily offered with all the content in the research class that also was customarily offered. This redesigned course used the same amount of time that the other two separate courses would have taken, but was explicitly built to work with both sets of ideas simultaneously.

We met every Thursday for an academic year from 9:00 a.m. to 3:30 p.m. We organized our day into five parts as follows:

- 9:00–9:30: Discussion of common themes across the assigned practice and research readings due for the day.
- 9:30–12:00: Mini-lecture on the research readings assigned for the day, looking for relationships to practice issues.
- 12:00–12:30: Students had lunch together and were encouraged to discuss course-related topics.
- 12:30–3:00: Mini-lecture on the practice readings assigned for the day, looking for relationships to research implications.
- 3:00–3:30: Discussion of crossovers between practice and research noticed throughout the day.

Initially, the students were puzzled and skeptical about the new course design because they believed that the two courses were entirely different and furthermore they detested the topic of research and thought this integration might intrude upon their practice class (which they tended to value). As we began, the students had a difficult time with the beginning and ending activities of the day. They had trouble detecting themes across the readings and seeing the areas of intersection between research and practice. We modeled for them what we could see for the first few meetings, and then, they engaged in an excited way with the exercise.

For example, in one of our first classes, we discussed the theme of "the power/value of a good question"—this theme was evident in both the practice and the research readings. Through a conversation between the two of us in front of the students, we explained how we used questions for inquiring into that which we were curious about and how the wording was important if we were interested in opening conversations and new possibilities. This idea was relevant both in the practice situation and in the research context. We asked each other questions about how this theme came to light for us, what "lenses" we were using in order to see this, what the implications might be for our practices, or what we might be missing by looking in this way. Through our conversation, we were demonstrating the crossovers we found in the readings as well as identifying them. Similarly, at the end of that day, we continued to model the kind of conversation we were hoping for in future classes.

Other crossover topics grew out of other readings on other course days. For example, early on, we talked about how as clinicians we try to understand what trouble a family is experiencing and would like to help with and as researchers, we are also trying to delve into a question or issue that no one has yet answered sufficiently. In both domains, we treat each case or issue as unique and yet part of a larger domain of understandings and knowledge from which to draw ideas that might be useful in any given instance.

The students worked with the same readings and activities that the customary classes included, but merging them in this larger format gave the students the perspective from which to see the interrelationships between research and practice. One of the most exciting days turned out to be the day that the reading assignments

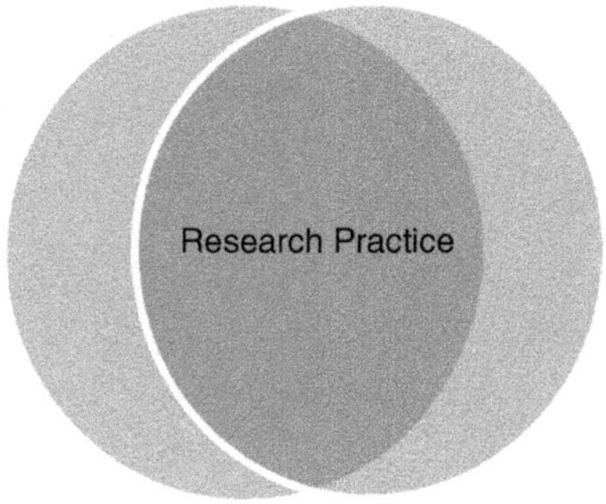

Fig. 3.2 The students worked with the same readings and activities

were on statistics (research) and coherence in a clinical session (practice). The students discussed the importance of being orderly yet flexible, being appreciative of "answers" and yet cognizant that what they were reading or hearing was a single story that cannot reveal all the complexities. They could see how research and practice tackled issues with similar commitment and interest even though they seemed to be different (Fig. 3.2).

Although initially reluctant, our students quickly became engaged and even excited with mixing practice with research. Toward the end of the academic year, they re-evaluated their initial assumptions about the differences between practice and research and made the following statement: "We don't even know if we can separate research and clinical work anymore, and if we could, we don't even know if it would be worth doing." We believe this marks a major professional transformation of teaching the role of the practitioner to be an active producer of knowledge along with stimulating behavioral change.

Research As Daily Practice

Subsequent to the research and practice course we mentioned above, we began to design how practice and research could be integrated in the field. We were convinced that it makes theoretical sense and could be conveyed successfully in the classroom, but could we work out the details to actually conduct the blend of the two in frontline practice?

We designed a way to blend practice and research that we call Research As Daily Practice (St. George et al. 2015b; Wulff and St. George 2014) that engages in "systematically examining our curiosities and information from our own clinical work in order to better understand what we *do* and, perhaps more importantly, what we *could* do" (St. George et al. 2015a). Basically, we are proposing a shift toward practice-based evidence (Fox 2003) with the notion of knowledge in action (Schön 1983) as primary. Evidence would come from the frontline of practice and that knowledge would be created and developed through application by practitioners themselves in the course of their daily work.

Fig. 3.3 The processes of doing practice and doing research side by side

By systematic we mean that the study is coherent with respect to a purpose, question of inquiry, data collection, and analysis (formally or informally). Importantly, it fits into what the therapist is already doing, rather than being something "extra." Our purpose in examining our practices and ways of seeing them as research is to be generative and future forming (Gergen 2014), that is, seeking to create possibilities of what "could be" instead of examining what is or was. Another intention was to encourage practitioners to value their experience and knowledge (and not feel that "researchers" had the only valid knowledge). The more we explored these interconnections, the more we began to see inquiry as the central process of how we, as therapists, practice every day. Presenting the actions of research and clinical work as one and the same set of processes, we believe that we are transforming practices and upholding the legitimacy and importance of both (Fig. 3.3).

We place the processes of doing practice and doing research side by side, each cast in their respective languages (Table 3.1).

We are also quick to acknowledge our worry about continuing the division of these two by utilizing this split vocabulary in this instance. Therefore, we have proposed, from a social constructionist perspective, a set of terms that point to a more inclusive set of processes from which these two sets (research and practice) emanate. This collection of processes suggests a way that human initiatives find meaning and, as such, may underlie what we have come to see as practice and as research (Table 3.2).

In many human endeavors, persons engage in processes that focus attention, follow that attention with attitudes of curiosity, engage in relationships with other

Table 3.1 The processes of doing practice and doing research side by side, each cast in their respective languages

Research	Practice
Select a question/hypothesis	Focus on a client or problem
Enlist participants and coresearchers	Engage with clients and stakeholders
Collect data and perform analysis	Create an assessment and treatment plan
Assemble findings and disseminate	Intervene and evaluate outcomes

Table 3.2 Collection of processes suggests a way that human initiatives find meaning

Attention
Curiosities
Relationships
Sense-making
Reflection in action

St. George et al. (2015b)

persons, pursue "making" sense of their situation and circumstance, and act on that knowledge.

Students quickly see the value in Research As Daily Practice with the emphasis on developing an understanding and then using that understanding to create plans or action steps. This is a pragmatic process that does not provide definitive or simple answers—but it does provide a coherent path to pursue. This helps beginning practitioners to ask the questions that concern them in their clinical work, engage with those most interested in asking and answering those questions, assemble information that could help answer the questions, figure out a reasonable way to make sense of the information, and then proceed in a concerted way. The word "research" would also fit the above series of steps.

For example, a student therapist working with couples who were relating in mean and disrespectful ways was unable to find relevant research (most research she found grouped all couple conflict together and her couples were not engaged in severe physical violence). She reinvented her therapeutic relationship to "interview" her client couples as would a traditional researcher. She asked questions without an interventive intent—she allowed her curiosity to understand what they were going through to guide her. Not only did she learn much more about their situations and experiences, she developed a less directive and interventive therapeutic style that she carried on in her professional career (Allen and St. George 2001).

In another example, beginning interns at the Calgary Family Therapy Centre (CFTC) wanted to learn how better to create "healing interpersonal patterns" (HIPs) from the corresponding "pathologizing interpersonal patterns" (PIPs). (In everyday language, HIPs represent the interpersonal patterns that family therapists encourage families to achieve. The PIPs are the troubling dynamics that families struggle with and attempt to change.) Creating HIPs becomes a basic skill at CFTC, and the interns were looking for effective ways to accomplish this. Given this concern, interns and supervisors constructed a project to notice various ways to develop HIPs. Focus groups were organized whereby the interns discussed early strategies to form HIPs, while the supervisors watched and took notes from behind the mirror. This was followed by the supervisors discussing with each other how they approached constructing HIPs in their practices and the interns watching from behind the mirror and taking notes. Creative use of resources and formats provided the interns with the opportunity to consider various pathways to create HIPs, and the supervisors had another tool to help them present the HIP material (Wulff et al. 2015b).

When considering rigor or validity of this process or outcomes, we use the following as a "criterion of goodness": "the degree to which research opens space for practitioners to change, creating something that was not there before" (St. George et al. 2015b). This process is interventive for the benefit of clients and their practitioners. We have provided details of three specific projects that we conducted at the CFTC elsewhere (St. George et al. 2015c; Wulff et al. 2015a, b).

The projects were based on a set of assumptions that were predicated on the idea that practice and research could be brought together in ways that enhanced practice and led to improved outcomes for clients. We found that these projects fit nicely into an agency structure by providing ways for practitioners to collaborate in examining the work they do within a framework that did not overtax the practitioners' time and resources. We also noticed a "spirit of curiosity and inquiry" emerge as practitioners had a bit more time to reflect on what they were seeing and doing with their clients across caseloads. This was an important outcome given the high demands on practitioners and agencies to produce large amounts of service hours with limited resources and time.

This process of "doing" research in practice allowed for many forms of methodologies and methods to be employed and fit nicely within already established practice patterns (Wulff 2008), supporting the notion that research processes are similar to competent practice patterns. Using Clarke's (2005) situational analysis, a visual form of grounded theory, we were able to investigate the relationships between PIPs and societal discourses (St. George et al. 2015c), an idea we had been discussing at CFTC for several years. The key here was that we modified the research project to fit with our own record keeping system of diagrammatically depicting family interactional patterns. We have also used narrative inquiry processes to tell stories of learning and teaching (Wulff et al. 2015b). Once the research terminology was modified into everyday language and commonsense understandings, it was fascinating to see how practitioners swiftly and deftly employed them. By translating them into the world of clinical or community practice, their utility was apparent and they become effective tools in the hands of practitioners.

Studying the processes in families and in the therapy itself led to immediate benefits in terms of practitioners regularly "trying out" new ideas that they were becoming aware of in their inquiries together. The gap in time for traditional research initiatives to be woven back into practices was bypassed in Research As Daily Practice, resembling action research whereby new insights were employed immediately, leading to new insights, and so on. There was also the sense of excitement associated with the practitioners' experience of creating new localized knowledge that would directly impact their work.

The monetary obstacle for agencies to produce research was removed by building the research process into agency activities and using agency personnel. Though practitioner time was used (in our case an hour per month), we bypassed a layer of bureaucracy and external requirements to meet funder expectations. This allowed the agency to create its own research agenda according to its timetables.

As practice embodies a flexibility, so too, did Research As Daily Practice have a flexibility that allowed the researchers to accommodate situations and opportunities that came up along the way. Oftentimes, unexpected invitations occurred that were "goldmines" for the research and being able to accept those deviations from the original plans proved critical for the success of the agency project. In our first Research As Daily Practice project at the Calgary Family Therapy Centre (see St. George et al. 2015c), we were able to shift our analysis given that the initial set of results did not effectively answer the questions we were posing. We had hoped to map two variables together to see how they were related, but given that there seemed to be no significant connection between them, we returned to the "drawing board" to see other ways the data and its analysis could inform practice. Out of this rethinking evolved a series of questions that were informed by the two variables we had hoped to see linked. These questions allowed us to achieve one of our research objectives which was to provide therapists with specific languaging by which they could encourage conversations about societal discourses in therapy.

The guidelines for Research As Daily Practice provide the practical basis for practitioner research to occur in frontline practice. The flexibility inherent allows for localized adaptations, but the centrality of the specific question and the practitioner (and agency) in the process remains constant. The activities involved are not so different from what practitioners already do, but the spotlight placed on the "researching" aspects of what they do seems to spur on these efforts. Students who hear our presentation and are shown the illustrations become energized about taking part or developing such projects in their own practicum work or at their places of employment. We have found that when practitioners sense that they are "researching" their practice or the problems their clients face, they welcome the inquisitive spirit into their practice that serves as a great antidote to feeling like one is just "going through the motions" or following a protocol.

Teaching Clinicians to Be Effective Consumers of Research

Another demonstration of linking research and practice is occurring in the graduate research course in our social work faculty. The attitude of many of the students is that the required research course serves no real useful purpose in their education—it is simply a requirement that must be met. Given this attitude, several years ago, the research teachers asked themselves, "How could a research course be relevant for graduate social work students whose career path was direct clinical practice?" An answer was to teach the students how to read and critically assess research articles for their potential value in adding to the practitioners' ability to assist their clients. Shifting the focus to teaching master's students to be excellent consumers of research helped us to reshape the research course that brought research and practice together in useful ways and changed students' pre-understandings and biases.

We present the idea of Research As Daily Practice in this class in the first couple of weeks to reinforce the idea that research and practice are very related. This helps set the tone for this course of approaching the idea of research in a more pragmatic fashion that is grounded in specifics that are relevant to social work practitioners. The course was built on a problem-based design in which the articles used (quantitative, qualitative, and mixed methods) generated the topics and issues that would be taken up in class for more detailed discussion. This format mirrored the practice context where specific situations or circumstances drive the knowledge needed by social workers. Rather than teaching decontextualized basic knowledge and then expecting real-world situations to use that knowledge, the reverse pattern is used—locate what is needed to know in a given situation (a client situation or in this research class, a given article that the student needs to understand) and then design learning to meet that challenge.

In appraising a quantitative research article, the students would be faced with methodological descriptions that went beyond their knowledge base. They might read that a regression analysis was performed. This would lead to their investigating what a regression analysis was in order to understand how that process was used in an effort to answer the questions posed in the research article. They would begin by seeing the research methodology in the context of its use and then the learning followed. Similarly, when reading a qualitative article that used "constant comparative analysis," questions arose and those served as the impetus to learn about constant comparative analysis. Seeing the methodologies or methods first presented in their applied form increased the students' interest in understanding them. The work on these research concepts or procedures continued until they could grasp the influence those concepts and procedures had in the context of the reported research.

Another similarity to practice is a need to "appraise" a situation, which means to look for both the weaknesses and the strengths. In the practice context, we look for a client's strengths or capabilities as well as times when problems or weaknesses occur. In these research article appraisals, the students need to find the value and usefulness of each article along with the article's shortcomings. Our experience in teaching this course is that students have been more adept at criticizing a research article than seeing its strength(s). Locating omissions or errors has value in reading research literature, but so, too, does looking for the utility of the article, the use of methods, and the findings/results.

Another learning component that fits well for practice is the need to *be specific* in supporting the statements that highlight strengths or weaknesses. The students are required to select quotes from the research articles that back up the assertions they make about the article. This helps the student stay focused on the specifics of what is being said and how it is being said (a good clinical skill as well).

These appraisal skills provide the student with the ability to thoroughly assess articles that their agencies may be considering implementing. We see it as our responsibility to prepare students to fully understand the research that is being used in agency work as evidence and justification to proceed in specific ways. Their appraising skills also make them excellent candidates to serve as reviewers for journal articles because the skills of article reviewing are not formally taught in graduate schools.

Our primary tool in facilitating article appraising is by having students first study and become familiar with an appraisal form/rubric (see Appendix) that we have developed and revised based on the Critical Appraisal Skills Programme (CASP 2013) and through conversations and projects with Ron Chenail at *The Qualitative Report* and in the development of a qualitative metasynthesis (Chenail et al. 2012). Studying the questions on this rubric guides students in learning the basic and expected content of quality research as revealed in research articles. They apply the rubric to three articles (quantitative, qualitative, and mixed methods), answering each rubric question and providing evidence to support their answers in the form of quotes from the article they are appraising. If they do not understand a particular statistical test, procedure, or vocabulary, they begin the search for that information on their own, in groups, or they bring the issue to class. The entire process of appraising a given article then takes on an atmosphere of an investigation, a process that is focused on an outcome but along the way, many new questions, ideas, and insights are brought forward. While most clinical master's programs teach students to be consumers of research, this research class makes this skill development the course focus. Research is not taught in a decontextualized way—research article appraisals are the vehicles to teach research methods and procedures. Students dig deeply into these articles and learn the elements of credible research (and what is not credible) as well as key components that could fuel their interest in conducting their own studies. Seeing the methods "in motion," that is, how they are implemented, reveals much more about the concepts than studying them in the decontextualized format of most research methods courses.

This way of teaching the research class has an advantage of quickly showing the students the relevance of research to their career path. They recognize the crucial role that "consuming" research articles can have in their careers. This demystification of research opens the door for students to engage with the idea of understanding an issue or situation without trepidation or concern that the topic is beyond them. Their enhanced self-confidence provides lots of energy to become genuinely curious about client situations and change, and this is a crucial attitude to possess for practitioners. Through this activity, the world of published research takes on a new importance to practitioners—something that is understandable and practical for their daily work.

Conclusion

We began with a set of assumptions about how practice and research were not inherently different. Our practices came into existence from a desire to erase the notion that research and practice are so specialized that they must be divided into component parts. Our speculation that such a distinction between practice and research offered ways of thinking could be useful, and at the same time, those distinctions closed down some ways of thinking that could also be useful. So we opened up that possibility in our thinking and to date, we have been working in the three ways we outlined in this chapter.

We are enthused by these projects and continue to work with them. Each project seems to spawn new versions of how they could be done. One idea that is making its way to the front now is how we might expand the ideas of practice and research (practice + research) to more actively include our clients. Another split we have been working with is between professional and client. We are now wondering about how useful that distinction is. What sorts of projects would evolve out of a blurring of the boundary about professional and client/layperson?

The heart of the idea of research for us has been the "burning curiosity" that researchers are reputed to possess. In 1996, we met Jack Horner, the renowned paleontologist in a museum/laboratory in Bozeman, Montana, where he worked. Horner gained attention when he hypothesized that dinosaurs were more akin to birds than to amphibians (Horner and Gorman 1988). He revealed to us his genuine curiosity that propelled him to form new theories about dinosaurs, but not with a sense of finality of uncovering the "truth." He saw his theorizing as providing a platform from which to think about dinosaurs and to provoke *new* thinking, not concretize current thinking (Wulff et al. 2000).

Similarly, we think therapists are well served when their curiosities lead them to new ways of thinking that open other pathways. We also believe that clients have the potential to have this sense of curiosity. Imagining therapists and their clients both engaging in mutual inquiry into what is happening in the clients' lifeworld has the potential to be transformative for the client, the therapist, as well as the larger community.

Appendix

Research Article Appraisal Questions

These 12 questions are prompts to help reviewers assess the quality of research articles (and the research the articles are based upon). In using these questions, feel free to expand each section in order to better focus on the specific aspects of the article you are assessing.

Initial Questions

1. **Is there a clear statement of the aims of the research?**
    - *What is the goal of the research?*
    - *Why is it important?*
    - *How is it relevant?*

2. **Is the type of methodology (quantitative, qualitative, mixed methods) chosen appropriate?**
   - *Does the researcher explain why he/she chose the methodology he/she did?*

More Detailed Questions

Research design

3. **Is the research design appropriate to address the aims of the research?**
   - *Is the chosen research design justified?*

Theoretical framework

4. **Is a theoretical framework for the research apparent?**
   - *Does the researcher explicitly connect the research to a theory base?*

Literature review

5. **Is there a literature review that contextualized this research?**
   - *Is the literature review broad enough?*
   - *Does the literature review reveal a knowledge gap?*

Sampling

6. **Is the recruitment strategy appropriate to the aims of the research?**
   - *Is the sampling strategy grounded in the literature?*
   - *Does the researcher explain how the participants were selected?*
   - *Is it explained why the selected participants were the most appropriate?*
   - *Does the researcher discuss why some people chose not to take part?*

Data collection

7. **Is the data collected in a way that addressed the research issue?**
   - *Is the setting for data collection justified?*
   - *Is it clear how data were collected?*
   - *Does the researcher indicate how the chosen methods of data collection were justified in the literature?*

- *Is it explained how the methods chosen were used?*
- *If methods were modified during the study, does the researcher explain how and why?*
- *Is the form of data clear?*

Reflexivity

8. **Is the relationship between researcher and participants adequately considered?**
    - *Does the researcher critically examine her/his role, potential bias, and influence?*
    - *Does the researcher make any changes during the study?*

Ethical issues

9. **Are ethical issues taken into consideration?**
    - *Is there evidence that ethics approvals were obtained?*
    - *Was there evidence that informed consent or confidentiality were included?*
    - *Was there evidence that any post-study effects on the participants were considered?*
    - *Was there evidence that ethical standards were maintained?*

Data analysis

10. **Is the data analysis sufficiently rigorous?**
    - *Is there an in-depth description of the analysis process?*
    - *Is the analysis process grounded in the literature?*
    - *Are there any illustrations of how the data were transformed through analysis?*
    - *Is there sufficient data presented to support the findings?*
    - *To what extent are contradictory data taken into account?*
    - *Is there evidence that the researcher critically examined her/his own role, potential bias, and influence during analysis and selection of data for presentation?*

Findings

11. **Is there a clear statement of findings?**
    - *Are the findings explicit?*
    - *Is there adequate discussion of the evidence both for and against the researcher's arguments?*

- *Does the researcher discuss the credibility of her/his findings?*
- *Are the findings discussed in relation to the original research question(s)?*

Value of the research

12. **How valuable is the research?**

    - *Does the researcher discuss the contribution the study makes to existing knowledge or understanding?*
    - *Does the researcher explicitly discuss the limitations of the study?*
    - *Does the researcher identify new areas where research is necessary?*
    - *Does the researcher discuss whether or how the findings can be transferred to other populations or consider other ways the research may be used?*

**At this point, you may sense that there are other qualities of research that need to be acknowledged that have not been adequately addressed by these 12 questions. Feel free to add more questions or sections that you believe are important to a fair and comprehensive appraisal of this article.
Adapted from the Critical Appraisal Skills Programme (CASP). (2013).

References

Allen, J. R., & St. George, S. (2001). What couples say works in domestic violence therapy. *The Qualitative Report*, *6*(3), 1–20. Retrieved from http://nsuworks.nova.edu/tqr/vol6/iss3/3

Chenail, R. J., St. George, S., Wulff, D., Duffy, M., Wilson Scott, K., & Tomm, K. (2012). Clients' relational conceptions of conjoint couple and family therapy quality: A grounded formal theory. *Journal of Marital and Family Therapy* [Special Issue], *38*(1), 241–264.

Clarke, A. E. (2005). *Situational analysis: Grounded theory after the postmodern turn*. Thousand Oaks, CA: Sage.

Critical Appraisal Skills Programme (CASP). (2013). *10 questions to help you make sense of qualitative research.* Oxford, England: Public Health Resource Unit. Retrieved from http://www.casp-uk.net/#!casp-tools-checklists/c18f8

Fox, N. J. (2003). Practice-based evidence: Towards collaborative and transgressive research. *Sociology, 37*(1), 81–102.

Gergen, K. J. (2014). From mirroring to world-making: Research as future forming. *Journal for the Theory of Social Behaviour*. doi:10.1111/jtsb.12075

Horner, J. R., & Gorman, J. (1988). *Digging dinosaurs: The search that unraveled the mystery of baby dinosaurs*. New York, NY: Workman.

Schön, D. A. (1983). *The reflective practitioner: How professionals think in action*. New York, NY: Basic Books.

Shaw, I., & Lunt, N. (2012). Constructing practitioner research. *Social Work Research, 36*(3), 197–208.

St. George, S., Wulff, D., & Tomm, K. (2015a). Research as daily practice: Introduction to the special section. *Journal of Systemic Therapies, 34*(2), 1–2.

St. George, S., Wulff, D., & Tomm, K. (2015b). Research as daily practice. *Journal of Systemic Therapies, 34*(2), 3–14.

St. George, S., Wulff, D., & Tomm, K. (2015c). Talking societal discourse into family therapy: A situational analysis of the relationships between societal expectations and parent-child conflict. *Journal of Systemic Therapies, 34*(2), 15–30.

Wulff, D. (2008). "Research/Therapy": Review of Adele Clark's. *Situational Analysis: Grounded Theory after the Postmodern Turn. The Weekly Qualitative Report, 1*(6), 31–34. Available at: http://www.nova.edu/ssss/QR/WQR/wqr1_6.html

Wulff, D., & St. George, S. (2014). Research as daily practice. In G. Simon & A. Chard (Eds.), *Systemic inquiry: Innovations in reflexive practice research* (pp. 292–308). London, UK: Everything is Connected Press.

Wulff, D., St. George, S., & Chenail, R. (2000). Searching for family therapy in the Rockies: Family therapists meet a paleontologist. *Contemporary Family Therapy, 22,* 407–414.

Wulff, D., St. George, S., & Tomm, K. (2015a). Societal discourses that help in family therapy: A modified situational analysis of the relationships between societal expectation and healing patterns in parent-child conflict. *Journal of Systemic Therapies, 34*(2), 31–44.

Wulff, D., St. George, S., Tomm, K., Doyle, E., & Sesma, M. (2015b). Unpacking the PIPs to HIPs curiosity: A narrative study. *Journal of Systemic Therapies, 34*(2), 45–58.

counselling-related experience. For the most part, however, entering into the therapy room with clients is a brand new experience for them. There is a lot riding on these first therapy sessions: Have I made the right vocational choice? Can I actually help people who are troubled and distressed? Am I learning what I came here to learn, and how will I know if I am? Will I get support from others when I need it? Will I be able to use my own skills and strengths?

Socially transformative family therapy practices are those which allow attention to and conversations about social influences on how persons interact, see themselves, consider change, and make meaning with regard to their current circumstances. With a view to supporting these practices from the beginning of therapy training, I (Lynda) design this course to emphasize therapists' attention to (a) the interactional nature of generative dialogue and therapeutic relationships and (b) historical contexts, social locations, dominant discourses, and structural influences affecting clients' and therapists' lives. It is a tall order to participate in and maintain awareness of interactions and relational processes in the therapy room while also considering structural and social influences on clients' lives and meaning-making. In addition, we ask therapists to attend to their own internal dialogue and assumptions. Add to this, for novice therapists, the self-consciousness that can accompany the performance of new tasks with high stakes, and these become somewhat daunting learning objectives (see Snyder, McIntosh, and Gosnell, Learning to Speak Social Justice Talk in Family Therapy 2015 for further descriptions of the challenges of engaging in this type of therapy talk).

Foundational skills for explicitly attending to social justice issues are those that allow new therapists to engage in generative dialogue, invite and utilize multiple perspectives, reflect on shifting and various dimensions of power and position, expand therapist self-awareness, and attend to social location and intersections (these foundational skills are also valuable in supporting practices described in St. George and Wulff, Community-Minded Family Therapy 2016). In the balance of this chapter, we will focus on how these skills can be effectively introduced by supervisors and utilized by novice therapists.

Engaging in Generative Dialogue in the Therapy Room

An intern therapist came to me (Lynda) reporting great distress after about 6 weeks of seeing clients. Admitting that her friends and family regarded her as a good listener and skilled conversationalist, she was questioning her choice of profession because she was finding the learning to be so hard. Expectations that engaging in generative dialogue should come "naturally" are not uncommon, and the unexpectedly steep learning curve can be disheartening. Supervisors at this juncture can acknowledge and appreciate the questions that arise and use this opening to invite deeper reflection on how therapy dialogue differs from ordinary conversation.

Generative dialogues are those which allow both client and therapist to consider the previously taken-for-granted or unquestioned aspects of clients' lives and as such form a central part of therapy practices directed towards discovering and considering broader social influences and injustices. The foundational skill of initiating such conversations is guided by models of dialogic therapy and a social constructionist perspective (see Andersen 1995, 2007, 2012; Bird 2002, 2004; Flaskas 2007; Gergen 2008; Levin and Bava 2012; Rober 2002; Strong and Tomm 2007; Wade 2007). It is grounded in therapists' ability to engage others with curiosity, openness, and attentiveness, in dialogue that focuses on meaning-making and understanding, as well as the relational interactions and systemic influences in people's lives.

Questions that encourage generative dialogue are those that invite more information and lengthier, more reflective responses. Utilizing the work of Karl Tomm as a starting point (Tomm 1988; Tomm et al. 2014), we engage in lots of group practice, asking each other questions and generating lists of potential questions to gain comfort in extending the conversation. For example, the group might consider various starting points in talking with a couple about their reported struggles with parenting—balancing information questions with questions that serve to "open space" (Anderson and Goolishian 1988) to consider expectations and daily lived experience. Diverse group suggestions and responses to each other build on therapists' cache of potential language, directions, and ways of taking up client responses.

While generating questions is an important skill, so too is careful listening—especially when attempting to step outside of one's own experience in order to hear about someone else's. We discuss the dangers of having too many ideas for next questions and failing to pause and be fully responsive to clients. Pauses between questions allow therapists to reflect on what they have heard and what perhaps seems unstated, while also providing clients with opportunities to add important detail and nuance. Group practice helps therapists gain comfort in waiting for the other and pausing for their own reflections.

It is valuable to recognize the types of responses that might be associated with questions that are "too different" or "not different enough" (Andersen 1995) such as a repeated "I don't know", brief responses, or physical shifting in the seat. This is also useful when preparing to ask questions that may feel a bit awkward for novice therapists themselves—for example, questions about class, sexual orientation, spiritual or religious beliefs, or history of trauma. We practise asking such questions with partners in the student group, gaining comfort with language, and moving from a broader or less explicit question (e.g., "Can you tell me if you have any particular beliefs or expectations that might be influencing your own experience of grief right now?") to more focused questioning (e.g., "Are there aspects of your Christian faith that you find helpful right now and other aspects that are not so helpful?"). Again, diversity in the peer group generates many examples of potential client responses and ways to use language in questions.

Conceptualizing relational interactions and broader systemic influences can be aided by using metaphors, tangible objects, or visual representations. Whiteboards and coloured markers, moveable miniature figures, and metaphors can focus supervision activities to engage therapists and supervisors in collaboratively understanding how the persons in the therapy room are responding to each other and how broader discourses, contexts, or assumptions might be seen.

Kelly responds: Early on, I found conceptualizing client interactions and generating hypotheses with respect to this to be challenging. Not only was the white board in Lynda's office a central piece to our supervision, it was also central to my developing these skills. Conceptualizing and mapping in this way left room for (a) those not present in the therapy room, but still influential in the therapeutic process (e.g., partners, parents, and children); and (b) present but sometimes less visible or prominent factors, such as substances, religion, trauma, values, and beliefs. What I most appreciated was the amount of "space" that the white board "opened up". The knowledge that I had the freedom to add to and erase pieces of my maps as my conversations with Lynda evolved, allowed me to feel safe sharing my thoughts—some of which were not fully formed until the marker connected with the white board.

Inviting and Utilizing Multiple Perspectives

A second foundational skill for considering social justice issues together with clients involves maintaining awareness of multiple perspectives on persons' lives and concerns, inviting these into the therapy dialogue, and using them to expand collaborative investigations of the various influences on clients' daily lives. Utilizing four different contexts for supervision (group, individual, dyadic, and reflecting teams) provides us with plenty of opportunities to consider therapists' own perspectives as well as those of others. Supervisors can introduce a particular perspective and invite alternatives, building skills in considering various perspectives and examining their implications. Taken-for-granted aspects of human and relational experiences can be demonstrated and challenged in a relatively homogeneous student cohort: "Since you are all young women with shared generational, class, or educational background, what do you think you might collectively be missing about this client's or family's current struggle with…?" Supervisors' own perspectives can introduce questions: "I come at understanding this couple's challenges in parenting teens from having done that fairly recently, and my own experience draws me to…; I wonder how you might hear this differently from your perspective of not being parents?" "What other experiences have you had that inform your listening to these parents?" Or questions can be introduced from an absent other (e.g., if no one in the supervision context is a father): "What do you think a colleague who is also a father might hear or see in this therapy interaction?" "How might he use his shared experience in understanding this father?" "What might you be able to do to bring a fathering ally more intentionally into the therapy room?"

Questions in dyadic supervision can explicitly draw on two therapists' perspectives. To Abby (therapist): What were you hearing in the room with this mother, and what stood out for you based on your own experience and possible assumptions about parenting teenage boys?

To Abe (supervision partner): As you view Abby's recorded therapy session, what stands out for you about the interaction between Abby and her client or what the client has to say? How do you think your own experiences and assumptions are influencing what you see and hear?

It may be easier for novice therapists to hear alternative ideas from peers than from supervisors. Supervisors can enhance these learning opportunities by interjecting, inviting clarification, or facilitating peer conversations. Reflecting teams provide a further means of sharing and highlighting multiple perspectives. Following the key ideas from Andersen's (1987) model, our first practicum teams consist of 3–4 peer therapists and a supervisor and include one or two opportunities for the observing team to share, in view of the client and therapist, reflections on what they are witnessing in the therapy session. Reflections are intended to be sufficiently diverse and tentative so as to open spaces for further client–therapist dialogue. In concert with the many positive aspects of working with reflecting teams, for both clients and therapists, that have been described by others (for a comprehensive review, see Chang 2010), we have observed specific benefits for novice therapists who are learning to work with multiple perspectives. These include enhanced opportunities to build skills in attending to and sharing one's own reflections; direct experience of how clients and therapists hear and utilize different perspectives; and exposure to a variety of ways to hear and see client–therapist interactions, as well as the multiple choice points and potential directions to follow in therapist–client dialogues.

Matthew responds: The reflecting team format offered a communally shared experience that underlined my learning in profound moments. During one reflecting team session, the client shared that hearing the team's appreciation for the ways the client was resisting the influence of depression was particularly helpful, and that hearing this from a number of individuals who were not the therapist validated the good job the client was doing. In our team debrief afterwards, I felt strongly connected to our team's shared witnessing of both this client's resilience and resourcefulness, and the client's moment of insight and positive affect expressed by face and words. I appreciated in a new way the power of being recognized for previously unacknowledged efforts, especially in the face of stigmatizing messages and interactions that often accompany experiences such as depression.

Reflecting on Shifting and Various Dimensions of Power and Position

A consideration of power is central to understanding and exploring issues of social justice in the context of clients' lives and the therapist client interaction.

Erica reflects: I recall that in my first practicum, I struggled with balancing a "not knowing" stance and finding my own presence and voice in therapeutic conversations. It was helpful to have conversations with Lynda that "not knowing" did not mean I did not know anything, but rather that my curiosity about clients' experiences was paramount in meaning-making together. I remember that, in this first semester of seeing clients, I really benefited from conversations that invited me to critically examine what was going on for me during therapeutic conversations that made it difficult for me to interject and be a more active participant in the dialogue. My fears of being perceived as dominant, "expert", and intrusive with my curiosity were significant for me to discuss in supervision, as these fears limited the expression of curiosity with clients. I remember that I had a conversation about this with Lynda, particularly around how my past experiences as a Child Protection Worker (CPW) left me fearful of being intrusive with clients in therapy. While I do not recall the exact wording of this conversation, I remember that Lynda invited me to consider how my discomfort with the power and authority inherent in my previous role might be interfering with me inserting myself more actively in conversations with therapy clients. I reflected that as a CPW, I was often required to ask what I considered to be rather intrusive questions of families in order to assess safety for children. As it is very important to me to be respectful and honouring of clients' stories, I was fearful that in my new role as a therapist intern, I would inadvertently be perceived as intrusive if I asked more questions Through this conversation, Lynda helped me explore the possibilities of expressing my curiosity about clients' stories while still deeply respecting their privacy and comfort: I recognised that there were many ways to ask questions respectfully, and that people were coming to therapy intentionally; I saw that if I did not participate actively in a dialogue with clients, then I might not be engaging in a way that was meaningful to them, and operating under a discourse of silencing.

A valuable starting point in considering the shifting dimensions of power and position with novice therapists is the influence of feelings of *powerlessness*. Often these are the most noticeable feelings and thoughts for new therapists. Relational, social constructionist and dialogic models of therapy discourage therapists from taking an expert position with regard to wholeness and health for clients, encouraging a more curious stance and avoiding certainty or diagnosis based on a knowledge base outside of the client's context. As Erica points out very nicely in her reflection, maintaining the practice of "not knowing" is challenging when you feel that you may not, in fact, know or be able to offer anything of value to your new clients. Feelings of powerlessness can lead to a therapist "overcorrecting" by being too withdrawn or too active with clients. In both cases, the effect may be that clients are unable to make a connection with the therapist or benefit from questions that invite alternative perspectives and meaning-making.

A sequence of questions for exploring these feelings might include the following:

- How do you think you respond in a situation in which others are depending on you and you are not certain about what to do?
- Do you think that this might be similar to how you will feel in this upcoming session?

- How will you notice that you are (talking too fast, saying very little) in response to these inner feelings of uncertainty, pressure to perform, or powerlessness?
- What do you think you could do differently when you notice this? How could you think about these feelings differently?
- How might you remind yourself of these new actions or thoughts? What would we see in a session recording if you are having success in addressing these feelings of powerlessness, anxiousness, or uncertainty?
- Would you be willing to have this conversation in the future as we review your work and look for the influences of this inner dialogue in your positioning in therapy sessions?

Similarly, supervisors and therapists can consider together how power and feelings of powerlessness may play out in supervisory relationships. For example, a supervisor might respond to a therapist's feelings of powerlessness by becoming more directive: "Because of the risk, and my responsibilities as a supervisor, we now need to talk about specific actions for you to take to ensure safety planning or informing authorities. While these actions are not optional, let's talk about what you need to feel supported and prepared to do what needs to be done to address these safety concerns. Can you also think of some ways that you can present this information to the client in order to acknowledge the lack of power he is feeling right now?"

Building on conversations about therapists' first-hand experience of powerlessness, supervisors can invite reflection on how clients may be experiencing feelings of powerlessness in therapy sessions and discuss how these feelings might affect the presentation, engagement, and language of persons in dialogue with each other.

Matthew responds: I also think about how feelings of powerlessness might invite interns and clients to overlook strengths and resources they do have, or omit or silence perspectives that might feel to be in conflict with the messages that tell them they are powerless (things they might "know"). Something else I really valued in our supervision conversations, and in ethics class, was the acknowledgement of institutional power assigned to therapists, even if they are interns, and how having an awareness of this power is helpful when we consider the possible unhelpful effects our "knowing" might have on clients.

The relative power assigned to persons based on socialized views of gender, age, skin colour, ethnicity, and ability (as examples) will influence interactions in therapy and supervision contexts. Sometimes, students who have primarily had discussions about power in classrooms have a sense that a person either has (and misuses) power or is powerless. It is perhaps more useful to consider power as a complex and shifting dimension of interactions. For example, a father enters into a first session very aware of the potential risk of losing access to his child if the therapist sees him in a certain way—the therapist is very powerful in that moment from the father's perspective and interactions between the two of them will likely reflect that. As the conversation continues, however, the father, who is also older than the younger female therapist, may begin to utilize gender and age privileges in interaction with the therapist. If we were to ask the two participants in this dialogue to reflect on their own feelings of powerlessness and the other's use of power, it is likely that they would each be able to identify the other's power and use of power at various points in time. Supervision conversations and reviewing therapy recordings can facilitate awareness of the changeable nature of power:

- As you watch this recording, what do you notice about how power shifts from moment to moment?
- What do you notice about how you act/talk when you feel as if you are holding more or less power?
- What do you notice about how the client appears to respond to feeling more or less power in the room?

Attending to the complex interactions associated with couple and family work means considering gendered, racialized, or parent/child voices in the room (e.g., "What messages about women are you hearing as these parents and their daughter talk together? I'm curious about what you made of the relative silence of the children during this discussion?"). Similarly, we can consider the potential for alignment or imbalance between participants and how this may privilege or silence certain individuals or perspectives (e.g., "If you were to place yourself in the son's shoes during this part of the session, what loyalties or constraints do you think might be silencing him?"). Role-playing in group supervision allows student therapists to take on positions that are different from their own social location based on age, family position, gender, class, education level, ability, and sexual orientation. For example, a student might be asked to take on the role of an unemployed mother or an immigrant Muslim adolescent, while others ask therapy-related questions or role-play other family members. Experiential exercises such as these allow for later reflection in response to questions such as

- What were you most aware of when you were asked…?
- What power, if any, did you feel that you had in the room? What surprised you about your response?
- How might this exercise change your own practice as a therapist?

Expand Therapist Self-awareness

Kelly reflects: Before returning to school for couple and family therapy, I held a position as a research coordinator for 5 years, during which time I had become accustomed to having the solution or knowing the right answer (e.g., knowing what statistical test to run, interpreting results, having solid numbers to draw conclusions). During my first practicum as a couple and family therapist intern, I found myself in a role where I felt incredible pressure to be the "expert", yet the answers were no longer readily available and objective. Lynda and I had multiple discussions throughout supervision about what it was like for me to leave this "privilege" behind: How was I going to be okay with not having the answers or solutions for clients? How was I going to sit across from an older male client and not be sure about what I was going to say next? I could not recall another time in my life where I had felt so incompetent.

What I most appreciated about Lynda's supervision is that she desired to know me in a way that would allow her to shape her supervision of my clinical work around me as a person. One striking example is the day Lynda asked me what it was like to be a teacher and practitioner of yoga. What does my practice ask of me and what do I teach my students? What would it be like to take those skills and implement them into my work as a therapist? Could I invite myself to be present for the moment-to-moment experience of the clients I sat with, rather than worrying about being one step ahead? And even if this was uncomfortable for me, if I were to breathe into the discomfort, as I would in any yoga posture, might this allow me to listen with an increased sense of calm and quiet, attending to and resisting the urge to nod my head and "m-hmm" with such frequency? Through Lynda's careful line of questions, I was able to recognize this as a physically embodied response to my discomfort sitting with the contradiction between uncertainty and perceived pressures to be the expert. Each time I sit with clients, I am thankful for Lynda's wise questions. If she had not taken the extra time required to "personalize" my supervision to me, I wonder how different my work as a therapist might be today.

Therapists' self-awareness provides an important base for orienting therapy work to social justice issues. Genuineness, thoughtful transparency, and drawing on one's own experience while remaining open to that of others aid in dialogues with clients about the influences of judgements, marginalization, shaming, and expectations in their daily lives. Kelly's thoughtful comments here, and those of other therapist interns, suggest that one way to support an expansion of therapist self-awareness is to explicitly draw on therapists' knowledge of themselves in supervision:

- How have you learned about certain areas of concern for clients, or ideas about healing/therapy/change?
- How is that learning influencing your understanding or actions in the therapy room and in supervision conversations?

These questions can also serve to guide self-supervision:

- What knowledge am I privileging here?
- Where else have I seen or heard or learned about this?
- What parts of myself am I allowing to have voice or to be silenced?

An equally important consideration, when supporting expanded self-awareness for therapists who are developing skills in attending to the complexities and injustices of people's lives, is the often intense emotional experience that can accompany the practice of therapy.

Matthew reflects: I recall reading articles by Flaskas (2007) *and* Weingarten (2010) *in my practicum class with Lynda on the varieties of ways to conceptualize, and interact with hope and hopelessness. As I reflect upon my experience as a new therapist-intern, the tensions described in these articles feel particularly relevant.*

Much as a client might hold feelings of both hope and hopelessness simultaneously, I feel that this is a good description of the dual positions I found myself in as a new therapist-intern. On the one hand, my hope was strong that I would not only learn through study, supervision, and practice to be of value to my clients in our therapeutic interactions, but that I would also avoid doing harm to them while I gained these skills. On the other hand, I also experienced strong feelings of hopelessness, especially with regards to my ability to be of therapeutic value to my clients as they brought a variety of presenting concerns and contextual realities to our work. In the absence of knowledge and experience, the complexity of therapy work sometimes felt overwhelming, and I found myself experiencing strong feelings of not having the necessary skills, such as where to lead our conversations and what questions to ask, or personal attributes to be of help to these clients. I brought these feelings of both hope and hopelessness to my supervision sessions with Lynda. Reflecting back on Weingarten and Flaskas' ideas of hope, I see their presence in Lynda's interactions with me. First, I identify strongly with Weingarten's concept of reasonable hope, and feel that Lynda was able to nurture the hope I felt through a reformulation of the expectations that comprised my "hopes". Lynda shared with me regularly the confidence that she had in my ability to do this work, and I found that this provided confirmation for my own hope. At the same time, Lynda routinely provided reflection of what she thought reasonable expectations of the therapeutic work that I would be able to do at this stage of my development might be. In the struggle between my own feelings of hope and hopelessness, I found that these sentiments helped me to lower my relative definitions of both success and failure. What it was that I hoped I would be able to do as a new therapist-intern seemed to become more manageable, which put less burden on my effort of hope. As the definition of failure became a more and more distant possibility for me, I found my feelings of hopelessness decreasing.

Why was the support that Lynda offered, and the result it had of helping me to manage the burden I had placed on hope, as well as the anxiety I felt due to felt sense of hopelessness, helpful for me as a new therapist-intern? Gaining a more "reasonable" feeling of hope allowed me to shed the chains of unreasonable expectations for myself in this early, vulnerable stage of my training, which I experienced as allowing me more freedom to feel excited at the opportunity to learn, and to feel less pressure to avoid failure.

Implicit for me in this experience of Lynda's supervisory support is the sense that my feelings of hope and hopelessness were two separate feelings, based on two separate thresholds, and that they both existed and were of value to process in supervision (Flaskas 2007). *This was important for me in particular in conversations where Lynda invited me to speak from my "worry". Being able to feel safe bringing my fears and worries into our conversation, and having Lynda engage with these feelings in a curious, and circular manner, helped me to embody my hopelessness, and through doing so, diminish its power over me.*

Matthew identifies the importance of being able to safely bring into supervision his struggles of how to be present with clients. In addition to creating a safe space, a generative supervision space is built on meeting therapists where they are, using the unique terms that make sense to them, and being willing to tolerate and explore in some depth the uncertainty, ambiguity, and both/and nature of intellectual, emotional, and physical experiences. Both Kelly and Matthew have reflected on the value of attending to the "embodied" experience of uncertainty, hopelessness, worry, feeling incompetent, and not having answers for clients. Asking about where and how these feelings are held and experienced within one's body (shakiness, fear, certainty, boredom) invites deeper therapist self-awareness.

Attending to and Reflecting on Social Location and Intersections

Kelly reflects: I remember one supervision meeting with Lynda that was particularly focused on social location and power. Likely trying to push me beyond my "go-to" gender and age differences, Lynda asked about my family history and background. Unlike the majority of my colleagues, I have come to realize that I know very little about my family lineage. My knowledge is limited to my awareness that my paternal grandfather is a first generation immigrant from the United States and my paternal grandmother a second-generation immigrant from Poland. I do not know how this impacted my father or how this might have impacted my own upbringing as a Caucasian female born and raised in Canada. There were no family stories or cultural narratives shared with me as a child—no rituals or traditions passed from one generation to the next beyond Halloween, Easter, and Christmas.

For several minutes, Lynda asked me to dig deeper, to find something about my family history that could be considered in terms of intersectionality with clients, how one or more aspects of background had shaped the person who was sitting in her office that day. And then, part way through this exploration, Lynda asked, "Is it possible that based on my own (Lynda's) social location and family background, I have assumed that you must know just as much about your historical lineage as I know about mine?" My (Kelly's) relief-filled response: "Yes"! I just grew up in a family in which no one got too excited about stories, traditions, church, or elections. For me, the more subtle aspects of social location still often feel hard to grasp and/or find evidence of existing in my own life.

Witnessing an individual in a position of power admit to making an incorrect assumption has been a rare experience for me. It was so humbling to hear Lynda acknowledge that she had done this, and admirable to observe her take ownership of her mistake and find the teaching opportunity available within it. Being a therapist does not mean you will be perfect. We all make incorrect assumptions and we all make mistakes. What is most important is that we actively strive to (a) identify our assumptions; (b) be intentional about what we do with them; and (c) maintain an awareness with respect to how they influence our work, whether this is with clients or supervisees. Can we acknowledge our assumptions or do we deny them? Can we take responsibility for our assumptions or do we become defensive? Can we find the opportunities for new perspectives and an opening up of space, or do we inadvertently or even intentionally close doors, constrain space and potentially disrupt the therapist-client (or therapist-supervisee) alliance? My experience was that Lynda supervises her students in a way that opens up, as opposed to closes off, space.

We use some in-class and written exercises in the practicum to facilitate therapists' understanding of their own social locations and potential intersections with clients. Hays (2008) describes aspects of context, identity, and social location with an ADDRESSING mnemonic (Age and generational influences, Developmental disability and/or acquired Disability, Religion and spiritual orientation, Ethnic identity, Socioeconomic status, Sexual orientation, Indigenous heritage, National origin, and Gender). Students identify their own social location based on these categories and discuss their insights and observations about this self-exploration with a classmate. Alongside more traditional genogram and eco-map conventions, intern therapists are invited to include ADDRESSING categories in initial and ongoing client "maps" that they prepare for each new client and adapt over the course of their work together, bringing these to each supervision consultation. We review together what therapists believe they know and do not yet know about the client's context and identity. This may lead to a discussion of what the therapist is curious about, or other people in the client's network who could be included in therapy sessions. Therapists reflect on areas of similarity or difference between themselves and clients and how these might influence their presumptions. Other considerations may include to whom in the client system the therapist feels more close or distant, or what inner voices or familiar pushes/pulls might influence the therapist in interacting with these clients.

When exploring these influences, I do not require or expect that therapists will disclose difficult or salient personal experiences in supervision. I do, however, invite therapists to reflect on how these may have a potential impact on the therapy room. When I ask these questions, I allow lengthy pauses for therapist reflection and then ask further questions about how these internal insights might be evidenced in interaction with clients. The questions I ask also provide a guide for questions that therapists can ask themselves during a session: What am I responding to? What might I be missing? How would I check that out? How is the client responding?

Near the end of the practicum, students complete an assignment that explicitly attends to the interface between therapist and client social location and context. They prepare for themselves a "map" of their own context and social location, and reflect on this in relation to a particular client, reviewing the client's map and transcribing a 20-minute segment of a recent therapy session with this client. In a column alongside the transcribed material, therapists provide notes about what they think was happening in the dialogue (therapist intentions, understanding of client intentions, opening/closing of space, types of questions, or positioning). In writing, they consider how areas of overlap, gaps, or intersections in social location between themselves and the client might challenge or enhance their therapy dialogue, what they might overlook, and how their own thinking or expectations about therapy with this client might be challenged. They also reflect on how the clients might describe these interactions differently and reflect critically on the processes of power, voice, and meaning-making in the transcribed segment of therapy. Finally, students reflect on how their own social location, values, and beliefs may have shaped their selection, analysis, and conceptualization of overall therapy work with this client. These various levels of critical reflection build and demonstrate skills in attending to self and other with a particular emphasis on interactions, diversity, privilege, and power.

Conclusion

We trust that we have provided here some food for thought and ideas that prove useful to your supervision practice (we direct the reader to Chap. 3, Wulff and St. George, Researcher as Practitioner: Practitioner as Researcher 2016 for ideas about engaging in inquiry as researcher and practitioner that would also enhance intern therapists' skills in questioning, listening, and inviting multiple perspectives). I (Lynda) want to thank Kelly, Matthew, and Erica for their reflections on their own experience and their contributions to various iterations of this writing. Our co-writing has provided a very generative dialogue in which some familiar and some new ways of considering supervision for new therapists have emerged. Similarly, it is through practice—engaging in supervision dialogue, reflecting on oneself as supervisor and therapist, working together with clients and others, stepping back and mapping the process, and considering what influences our own perspectives and what shapes clients' lives and our therapy discussions that we gain further understanding and appreciation for the complexities of therapy (for more examples of the potential benefits of "softening" rather than "hardening" categories as a learner, see Chenail, Gordon, Willson, and Pantaleao, Everyday Solution-Focused Recursion 2016). These first steps into a supervisory dialogue and learning to be a therapist provide lots of opportunities for profound engagement with each other and with foundational ideas that will shape our work (as supervisors and as therapists) for a long time. As such, it is an immense privilege for supervisors to enter into this familiar and unfamiliar territory, requiring careful attention to challenging and encouraging the complexities of power and learning processes, and our social and relational contexts. It should feel at least a little bit risky and a little bit humbling—this is why we do it together.

References

Andersen, T. (1987). The reflecting team: Dialogue and meta-dialogue in clinical work. *Family Process, 26*, 415–428.

Andersen, T. (1995). Reflecting processes: Acts of informing and forming. In S. Friedman (Ed.), *The reflecting team in action* (pp. 11–37). New York, NY: Guilford.

Anderson, H. (2007). A postmodern umbrella: Language and knowledge as relational and generative, and inherently transforming. In H. Anderson & D. Gehart (Eds.), *Collaborative therapy: Relationships and conversations that make a difference* (pp. 7–21). New York, NY: Routledge.

Anderson, H. (2012). Collaborative relationships and dialogic conversations: Ideas for a relationally responsive practice. *Family Process, 51*, 8–24.

Anderson, H., & Goolishian, H. (1988). Human systems as linguistic systems: Evolving ideas about the implications for theory and practice. *Family Process, 27*, 371–393.

Bird, J. (2002). *The heart's narrative: Therapy and navigating life's contradictions*. Green Bay, NZ: Edge.

Bird, J. (2004). *Talk that sings: Therapy in a new linguistic key*. Auckland, NZ: Edge Press.

Chang, J. (2010). The reflecting team: A training method for family counselors. *The Family Journal: Counseling and Therapy for Couples and Families, 18*, 36–44. doi:10.1177/1066480709357731

Flaskas, C. (2007). Holding hope and hopelessness: Therapeutic engagements with the balance of hope. *Journal of Family Therapy, 29*, 186–202.

Gergen, K. (2008). Therapeutic challenges of multi-being. *Journal of Family Therapy, 30*, 335–350.

Hays, P. A. (2008). *Addressing cultural complexities in practice: Assessment, diagnosis, and therapy* (2nd ed.). Washington, DC: American Psychological Association.

Levin, S., & Bava, S. (2012). Collaborative therapy: Performing reflective and dialogical relationships. In A. Lock & T. Strong (Eds.), *Discursive perspectives in therapeutic practice* (pp. 126–142). Oxford, United Kingdom: Oxford University Press.

Rober, P. (2002). Constructive hypothesizing, dialogic understanding, and the therapist's inner conversation: Some ideas about knowing and not knowing in the family therapy session. *Journal of Marital and Family Therapy, 28*, 467–478.

Strong, T., & Tomm, K. (2007). Family therapy as re-coordinating and moving on together. *Journal of Systemic Therapies, 26*, 42–54.

Sutherland, O., Fine, M., & Ashbourne, L. (2012). Core competencies in social constructionist supervision? *Journal of Marital and Family Therapy, 39*, 373–387. doi:10.1111/j.1752-0606.2012.00318.x.

Tomm, K. (1988). Interventive interviewing: Part III. Intending to ask lineal, circular, strategic, or reflexive questions? *Family Process, 27*, 1–15.

Tomm, K., St. George, S., Wulff, D., & Strong, T. (Eds.). (2014). *Patterns in interpersonal interactions: Inviting relational understandings for therapeutic change*. New York, NY: Routledge.

Wade, A. (2007). Despair, resistance, hope: Response-based therapy with victims of violence. In C. Flaskas, I. McCarthy, & J. Sheehan (Eds.), *Hope and despair in narrative and family therapy* (pp. 63–74). New York, NY: Routledge.

Weingarten, K. (2010). Reasonable hope: Construct, clinical applications, and supports. *Family Process, 49*, 5–25.

Chapter 5
Learning to Speak Social Justice Talk in Family Therapy

Lynda J. Snyder, Shannon McIntosh and Faye Gosnell

Learning to Speak Social Justice Talk in Family Therapy

Family therapists are encouraged to integrate principles of social justice into their daily practice (Thomas 2003). Interns are expected to learn the skills necessary to incorporate social justice talk in their work with families. But what kinds of conversations and activities help family therapists expand their understandings of social justice and enhance their efforts to implement these understandings in their work with families? The purpose of the study discussed in this chapter is to respond to this question.

This study was conducted at the Calgary Family Therapy Centre (CFTC) in Calgary, Alberta, using a practitioner-based inquiry process referred to as Research As Daily Practice (St. George et al. 2014). Research As Daily Practice involves still-evolving knowledge and values the potential for meaning-making present within diverse perspectives. These research principles are important as practitioners at CFTC value and integrate multiple philosophical and theoretical viewpoints in their daily practices. For example, Dr. Karl Tomm, the founder and program director of the Centre, states his work has been informed by various theoretical perspectives over the time of his practice (e.g., von Bertalanffy's systems theory, Bateson's ecology of the mind, Maturana's bringforthism, and more recently Gergen's social constructionism). The influence of these theoretical perspectives, in particular social constructionism, can also be seen in this study.

Social constructionism (Lock and Strong 2010; Paré 2014; Tomm 2014) situates the locus of change in therapy within the relational interactions that occur over the

L.J. Snyder (✉) · F. Gosnell
Calgary Family Therapy Centre, Calgary, AB, Canada
e-mail: lyndajoysnyder@hotmail.com

S. McIntosh
Alberta Health Services' Child and Adolescent Addictions and Mental Health, Specialized Services, Calgary, AB, Canada

S. St. George and D. Wulff (eds.), *Family Therapy as Socially Transformative Practice*, AFTA SpringerBriefs in Family Therapy,
DOI 10.1007/978-3-319-29188-8_5

course of the therapeutic process. These interactions can be constructed in ways that are "generative, socially just, and collaborative" (Lock and Strong 2010, p. 305) or in ways that capture families and therapists in restrictive practices. Paré (2014) refers to this type of limiting dialogue as a form of *therapeutic injustice*, a concept that is evident in the findings of this study.

Strong (2014), an academic and family therapist associated with the Centre, reminds us that "humans [as interpretive beings] selectively attend to what is in their circumstances. How they interpret such phenomena…typically owe[s] something to prior experiences (including forms of training)" (p. 44). This idea is important when considering the meaning-making practices involved in research endeavors—including this project. Those involved in this project come from different professional disciplines and have varying life experiences. The interplay between the participants and the authors of this study, and the knowledge constructed during this research endeavor, reflects nuances of our diversity.

Lynda's perspectives are influenced by her training as a clinical social worker and marriage and family therapist. She has been a clinical supervisor for 20 years and has mentored family therapists, psychologists, social workers, psychiatrists, and nurses. Lynda is Canadian-born but has lived and worked in five countries. Her understanding of social justice has been colored by living in two countries impacted by civil war and her work with families impacted by political upheaval and relational violence.

Shannon is a registered social worker who has a master of social work degree from the University of Calgary. She is also a wife and mother of three children. Shannon's fascination with social justice stems primarily from her work with families who have been impacted by mental health struggles, oppression, and stigma. Through this experience and while writing numerous articles on family matters as a freelance writer, Shannon has become more attentive to the impact social discourses have on families and how these expectations can pose unrealistic pressures that compound stress and mental illness. These issues inspired Shannon to complete a case study on social justice in family therapy during her internship at the CFTC. Shannon is also very passionate about the potential of art and music in facilitating healing of those hurt by social injustices.

Faye Gosnell is a White Master's student in her mid-30s. After taking time out of the workforce to focus on motherhood, she is now completing her master's studies in counseling psychology. Faye's interest in social justice relates largely to her experiences living in rural communities in eastern Canada. She has worked in a volunteer capacity to address issues of intimate partner violence in these communities. She has also experienced firsthand the various social pressures related to single motherhood. Faye has always been fascinated by the relationship between discourses about the so-called successful living and the realities that tend to arise when viewing success and its "legitimate" pathways in such constraining ways.

All three authors participated in all phases of this study. Lynda provided leadership for the project, facilitated the focus groups, analyzed the information gathered, and compiled this chapter. Shannon and Faye participated in the study, analyzed the findings, completed the literature review, and reviewed and contributed their ideas to the writing of this chapter. Another research participant also contributed to the analysis and thematizing of the information gathered during this project. All together, 10 family therapy interns and 2 clinical supervisors were involved in this work, in which we explored the kinds of conversations and activities that support family therapists in expanding their understandings of social justice and enhancing their abilities to implement these in their work with families. Micro-practices reflected in these learning activities are identified and related to the development of practitioners' understandings of social justice and family therapy. A discussion regarding the potentialities of family therapy as a mode of socially transformative practice concludes this work.

Social Justice: Concepts and Practicalities

Clinical social workers (Hair 2014; Helms 2003; McLaughlin 2009), counseling psychologists (Ivey and Collins 2003; Rupani 2013), and family therapists (Seedall et al. 2014) identify social justice as an important ideal. However, the philosophical complexities (Harrist and Richardson 2012) and practicalities involved in integrating this concept into daily practice can be challenging (Greene 2005; Hair 2014; Ivey and Collins 2003; Kakkad 2005; McLaughlin 2009, 2011; Rupani 2013; Seedall et al. 2014; Vallejos-Bartlett 2003).

For the purposes of this study, social justice is conceptualized as involving three distinct but overlapping elements (McLaughlin, 2011). The first element, *social systems*, is perceived to be in place to "facilitate the well being of community members and dispense social justice" (p. 240). Social systems include political and economic systems as well as more "intimate systems such as the health care system, the child welfare system and the family system" (p. 240). The second element is *people's ability to access resources* in a fair and equitable manner. Resources include shelter, food, material resources, and discretionary services and opportunities. The third element of social justice is *transformative respect,* a resource "conveyed through deeply held beliefs and attitudes toward others actively conveyed through language and action" (p. 242). Transformative respect is also perceived as the interpersonal medium through which clinicians enact their beliefs and values including respect, the right to self-determination, and a commitment to equality.

Therapeutic conversations are thus seen to be "a venue for the enactment of social justice" (Paré 2014, p. 215). Paré expands the concept of resources, mentioned in McLaughlin's (2011) work, to include "the *diversity of potential accounts* from which clients may draw on in making sense of their lives" (p. 18). This concept is particularly relevant when considering social justice talk in family therapy from a social constructionist perspective. It is my experience (Lynda) that families frequently enter therapy with a negative and/or constrained perspective of themselves and their interactions. Alternatives and exceptions to oppressive and unjust practices may never have been explored or perceived by these families as viable ways of relating. Thus, providing families with a diversity of potential accounts for making sense of their lives can be a forum for challenging injustices and creating opportunities for change within family systems.

Tomm (2014) also upholds therapeutic conversations as an essential forum for the pursuit of social justice and upholds this pursuit as an *ethical imperative*. He states:

> It is unethical to simply stand by and do nothing about social injustices. . .What seems far more ethical to me is that we, as therapists, try to live congruently and prevent or reduce injustice whenever we can, both inside and outside of therapy. (p. 239)

While the principle of social justice is upheld by many family therapists and addressed in counselor training programs (Thomas 2003)—including the training offered at the CFTC (Tomm 2014)—Thomas points out that, "the intersection of social justice and Marriage and Family Therapy (MFT) [can] be…a gridlock or (worse) an accident site, depending on the training program" (p. 34). Paré et al. (2004) further suggest that counseling interns can experience a sense of vulnerability during their time of training and that training can be "a time of humility, if not humiliation, when the gap between intentions and results is often glaringly evident, and much energy is expended on self-evaluation and critique" (p. 118) and learning activities can be "a public forum for public dismissal and shaming" (p. 119). Nevertheless, others describe the conversations interns engage in during training as affording opportunities for generativity and the witnessing of success (Chang and Gaete 2014; Paré et al. 2004; Wulff and St. George, Researcher as Practitioner: Practitioner as Researcher, 2016).

In this study, we explored the activities and practices family therapy interns at the CFTC found supportive of their endeavors to understand social justice and its relationship to family therapy. We used a Research As Daily Practice (St. George et al. 2014) approach, which integrated Reason's (1998) four phases of cooperative inquiry (CI). The four phases included: Phase One, Conceptualization and Initial Engagement; Phase Two, Collaborating and Clarifying Research Plans; Phase Three, The Gestation Period; and, Phase Four, Analysis and Synthesis. A brief description of each phase is provided below.

Phase One: The Conception of This Study and Initial Engagement

The conception of this project took place within the practice setting of the participants and the authors. It occurred shortly after Sally St. George and Dan Wulff introduced their interest in engaging the family therapy interns and staff at the CFTC in a Research As Daily Practice project focusing on **how** *social justice talk* (Paré 2014) can be integrated into family therapy. Everyone thought Sally and Dan's research proposal sounded interesting, empowering, and presented an opportunity for participants to enhance their knowledge and skill regarding social justice talk in family therapy. Nevertheless, conversations in the kitchen, the workrooms, and the Centre's hallway suggested that while social justice was upheld as a valuable ideal, few felt confident in their understandings of this principle and their abilities to operationalize this concept in their practice with families. This confusion and uncertainty prompted me (Lynda) to wonder about what types of conversations and activities family therapists and interns find helpful in expanding their understandings of social justice and supportive of their efforts to integrate social justice talk in their work. I began asking others what they thought and somewhere between the intern workrooms and the Centre kitchen this study was conceived, and the following research question was born: "*What kinds of conversations and activities help family therapists expand their understandings of social justice and enhance their efforts to implement these understandings in their work with families?*"

Phase Two: Collaborating and Clarifying Research Plans

Informal conversations about social justice and family therapy continued, and after several weeks, a meeting to further discuss this study was organized. During this first group discussion, the research question and a proposed research methodology were discussed. The participants agreed to meet twice more to discuss their learnings. The three group discussions resembled focus groups integrating a non-directive interview format (Kvale and Brinkmann 2009) and were facilitated by Lynda. A critical decision made by the participants during these meetings involved them reviewing the journals they had written as part of their coursework in which they discussed their learnings regarding social justice talk in the practice of family therapy. These accounts became a substantive portion of the information gathered in this study.

Phase Three: The Gestation Period

During the third phase of this study, family therapy interns immersed themselves in the CFTC's family therapy training program. This involved conducting counseling sessions with families, participating in clinical supervision, observing each other's work, and engaging in lively discussions about what they were learning. Each week, the interns and staff therapists participated in a five-part screening session consisting of a pre-session conversation, an interview with the family, a reflection offered by members of the reflecting team, a conversation with the family regarding what they heard the team discussing, and a post-session conversation among the interns, therapists, and the consultant. Frequently, these post-session conversations included social justice talk. Once a month, the weekly screening was followed by a research meeting. During the period of time considered in this study, the research meetings centered primarily on Sally and Dan's study on *how* social justice talk occurs during family therapy sessions. The study discussed in this chapter was not specifically addressed during these meetings, which created an opportunity for participants to consider how joining in Sally and Dan's research project did or did not support their developing awareness of social justice and family therapy.

During Phase Three of this study, many of the participants also attended university classes where social justice talk occurred as people asked questions, puzzled together, and reflected on their evolving understandings of social justice and their work with families. Many of the participants recorded their learnings in their journal entries. Two postgraduate interns wrote personal reflections, which were later submitted as part of the data analyzed in this study.

Phase Four: Analysis and Synthesis

In Phase Four of this study, a literature review was conducted and the third and last group discussion was held near the end of the interns' 8-month training period. At this meeting, the participants identified and discussed numerous moments of learning about social justice they saw as particularly significant. This information was recorded and subsequently analyzed along with the journal entries submitted by the participants. Four reviewers independently read each account and identified learning moments and micro-practices they saw associated with the learning activities discussed by the participants. The reviewers then submitted their findings to Lynda who reviewed and aggregated the accounts using the categories of learning activities and micro-practices identified. The findings were synthesized into the following account. The writing of this chapter concluded the fourth and final phase of this project.

Findings: A Synthesis of Learnings About Learning

In this study, participants described their learning about social justice and family therapy as a social/relational activity that involved the development of knowledge through dialogue with others and oneself. Learning involved reflective and reflexive practices which occurred in a variety of settings. In this study, *reflective practices* were described as moments when participants were able to step back and consider their understandings of possible power dynamics within relationships and potential intersectionalities between family dynamics and oppressive practices relating to systemic racism, financial privilege, gender accounts, and the marginalization of families within larger social systems. The importance of reflective practices is illustrated in the following quote: "I am learning to manage social justice conversations through suspending [or holding] my thoughts and refraining from making immediately false or unethical judgements. I feel this requires persistence and emerging into an internal dialogue with myself."

Journaling was also described as a form of reflective practice and was identified as an important activity participants used to capture and reflect upon their learnings. "The posts function to trigger my memory of in-session events," one participant stated.

Reflexive practices were described as moments during which participants considered their positionality and ways of interacting and how these might influence the response of others. Reflexive practices were seen as occurring during training and during clinical practice. For example, one of the participants commented:

> When I am talking to colleagues, supervisors, or participating on reflecting teams I am attuned to the moments when people gently ask how a person came to forming and adopting the beliefs they hold. . .This has been a huge sparkling moment for me, in regards to how I engage social justice themes in therapy. I have begun to ask my clients about their belief systems, while maintaining my curious stance. From this place of curiosity, I am able to elicit critical reflection which contributes to the deconstruction of social justice issues within the therapy context.

As illustrated above, transitioning one's awareness of social justice into one's therapeutic practice was considered to be a critical aspect of clinical training. However, the effects of listening to accounts of social injustices affected the therapists and sometimes their responses within a session. This dynamic can be seen in the following reflection.

> During a session with an immigrant couple who had not communicated with one another for months, the husband shared that he was afraid of engaging in difficult conversations with his wife for fear that he would raise his voice, would then be heard by neighbors, reported to authorities, and then taken to jail. The husband also noted that he felt Canada was "a place for women and children" and that men were unfavored. *Upon hearing this I was immobilized by his comment. This emotional response stalled the flow of the conversation* [emphasis added].

This participant goes on to describe how she engaged in a conversation with the members of the reflecting team for this session, her supervisor, and her colleagues in order to explore alternative approaches to working with families encountering social injustices. The open communication among this participant and her colleagues reflects the importance of developing supportive learning communities in which participants' roles are flexible (Chenail, Brett Gordon, Wilson, and Pantaleao, Everyday Solution-Focused Recursion: When Family Therapy Faculty, Supervisors, Researchers, Students, and Clients Play Well Together, 2016).

Another participant shared a similar concern: "My greatest challenge has been to maintain a position of curiosity and compassion with people who may perform certain oppressive practices, while opening space for them to step into accountability." Learning to maintain the therapeutic relationship while managing social justice conversations was portrayed as a primary learning objective by the participants and their commitment to learning ways to address this challenge is portrayed below.

> During my time at the Centre, I have struggled to find ways of making oppressive discourses visible through conversation with families, while at the same time maintaining the engagement of those who stand to benefit most from the enactment of these discourses. This skillful dance is a delicate balance that, to me, remains a constant source of refinement and interest in my learning.

Another participant described the tensions she experienced while trying to learn how to maintain the therapeutic alliance and simultaneously engage in social justice talk. She stated:

> During one of our initial sessions, the stepfather alluded to some beliefs regarding gender such as "women are emotional, irrational and sensitive" and men are "logical and rational." I attempted to deconstruct these discourses . . .Unfortunately. . the stepfather was not open to this exploration and *I felt personally impacted as a female regarding the perceived injustice I was witnessing* [emphasis added].

Following the session, the therapist talked with Dr. Tomm, who agreed to provide a consultation with the family to "further explore and deconstruct the injustices of gender." The therapist reported she appreciated his assistance but stated she also continued to question if her gender as a woman might at times restrict her ability to create change in the therapeutic process and address larger macro-level issues of oppression, power, and privilege in practice. She asked, "If I was a male, would I require a consult from a male colleague to address oppressive discourses about gender?"

Collectively, these examples illustrate some of the challenges encountered by participants while learning about social justice and family therapy. They also identify micro-practices that support learning and illustrate the importance of engaging in internal and external dialogues that support the development of reflective and reflexive practice (Chang and Gaete 2014; Paré et al. 2004). The following quote captures the significance of engaging in learning activities that provide multiple opportunities to develop reflective and reflexive practices.

> Starting off in the MSW program I struggled to understand how social justice and therapy mix. Through countless discussions with supervisors, professors, colleagues, and friends I have come to the understanding that social justice work in therapy is when I give voice to the social discourses of power, privilege, and oppression. . .when I am talking to colleagues, supervisors, or participating on reflecting teams I am attuned to the moments when people gently ask about how a person came to forming and adopting the beliefs they hold. . .I have begun to ask my clients about their belief systems, while maintaining my curious stance. From this place of curiosity, I am able to elicit critical reflection, which contributes to the deconstruction of social justice issues within the therapy context.

These accounts also remind us of the multiple intersections of inequalities (Seedall et al. 2014) that exist at the individual, family, institutional, and societal levels. In the following excerpt, several intersections of injustices are identified and the participant's emerging understandings of ways to address these oppressive practices are expressed.

> Social justice talk in therapeutic conversations mediates between oppression at the personal level and oppression at the structural level. . .We begin by exploring the experiences and feelings behind experiences of injustice, and then go on to question what structural ideas

> are in place that support such injustices, what purpose they hold, how the clients are protesting them, and who the clients have to support them in their endeavors. . . .Exploring the supports clients have in their lives also creates opportunities for establishing solidarity for collaborative action. . .The clients themselves become the agents of change, which empowers them and works against their experience of oppression.

Another participant described how she was inspired by the potential for collective action evidenced within the members of the interdisciplinary team practicing at the Centre. She stated:

> I have been privileged to work with a multidisciplinary team, including educational counsellors, social workers, psychologists, and psychiatrists. When I first joined the team, I saw. . .an opportunity to learn about our differences. . . . Surprisingly, I have actually found more similarities between us than differences.

Discussion

Family therapy provides a potential forum for socially transformative practice as social justice talk is effectively incorporated into therapeutic conversations with families. A social justice perspective in family therapy considers how historical and present structures and beliefs perpetuate and grant entitlements to some groups at the expense of others (Seedall et al. 2014). The perpetuation of these inequalities is often taken-for-granted and maintained in ways that restrict possibilities for alternative, growth-enhancing interactions within families. Social justice talk creates opportunities for families to sort through socially endorsed explanations and access alternative accounts as they co-construct their preferred identities and relationships (Paré 2014).

Learning how to navigate social justice conversations was described by the research participants as a challenging but critical endeavor. This type of therapeutic conversation seemed to create opportunities for social change on multiple levels. Learning activities that provided opportunities to engage in internal and external dialogues that supported the development of reflective and reflexive practices were described as supporting the participants' efforts to expand their understandings of social justice and its relationship to family therapy. The importance of creating collaborative learning communities was also cited as important by Ashbourne, Fife, Ridley, and Gaylor, Supporting the Development of Novice Therapists. Learning within a multidisciplinary setting in which professionals from different disciplines upheld and integrated social justice talk in their practices was further seen to create a solid foundation for collective action toward a more just society.

Participants also identified the importance of leadership in modelling social justice in their daily practices. These practices included supervision, clinical consultations, and the relationships leaders had with others inside and outside of therapy sessions. Engaging in generative conversations that embody *transformational respect* and invite reflection and reflexivity was seen to be essential in the development of the knowledge and skills required to engage in effective social justice talk.

Finally, the participants in this study saw social justice talk in family therapy as a potential mode of social action. Consciousness-raising was described as an important first step to social action in both training and family therapy. The importance of training as a means of consciousness-raising for family therapy interns is captured by an international intern studying at the Centre.

> I have had lots of opportunities to observe, be part of reflective teams, etc. and these opportunities have helped me learn more about social injustices. . . .I have found that the more I learn about social injustice, the more I find this issue coming up.

Recognizing social injustices is an important first step in catalyzing social action. But therapists cannot stop there. They need to move beyond acknowledging the existence of injustices to being able to engage families in social justice talk that brings about social change. Learning these skills takes commitment and effort by agencies and interns. But, the participants in this study see this as a worthy goal and believe that when family therapists learn to engage in social justice talk that leads to families relating in ways that contribute to a more just society, this is socially transformative practice—one family at a time!

Conclusion and Key Learnings

In this study, social justice is considered to be multifaceted involving three distinct but overlapping elements: *social systems*, one's *ability to access resources*, and *transformative respect* (McLaughlin 2011). Family therapy is seen to be a potential venue for the enactment of social justice (Paré 2014; Tomm 2014). Participants describe the importance of engaging in a variety of learning activities that provide opportunities for meaningful internal and external dialogues. These dialogues are seen to be generative when they are built upon transformational respect and provide family therapists with diverse accounts and experiences to draw upon as they develop their understandings of social justice and hone the skills required to integrate social justice talk into family therapy.

In conclusion, each of us (Lynda, Shannon, and Faye) has garnered key learnings from this study. Faye and Shannon comment that an important takeaway for them is the idea of embracing vulnerability in discussions about social justice: both one's own and that of others. Faye states:

> As students of family therapy, we may navigate issues of social justice apprehensively out of a fear of imposing inadvertent biases on our clients. No therapist-in-training wants to think of him or herself as "oppressive" and thus, the temptation to shy away from difficult questions may be strong, particularly if we fear the therapeutic alliance may suffer from broaching a nuanced issue. It can be hard to know when and how to skillfully "call out" the tacit assumptions that may be operating in our clients' discourses. Given these challenges, there is great benefit in engaging both clients and colleagues in discussions about our nuanced understandings of the meanings of social justice.

Shannon further reminds us that holding a sense of tension between the emotions inherent in social justice discussions and embracing the trust that can develop therapeutically with families requires stamina of both will and heart.

For Lynda, as a clinical supervisor, two critical learnings stand out from this study. Firstly, the importance of agency personnel at all levels upholding transformational respect as a principle of social justice is paramount. Secondly, the importance of acknowledging the complexities present for those seeking to expand their understandings of social justice and enhance their skills in integrating social justice talk into practice cannot be overlooked. The participants in this study identified feelings of vulnerability both in and out of the counseling room. However, they also indicated a strong desire to uphold principles of social justice in their work with families. Creating opportunities for dialogues in which these complexities can be openly discussed needs to be incorporated into all of an agency's learning activities. Developing a safe and protected environment in which interns and therapists can explore their thoughts and experiences relating to social justice talk in family therapy needs to be actively pursued in our education and training of family therapists.

Finally, this study has led all of us to conclude that engaging in social justice talk with families can be a mode of socially transformative practice that can contribute to the development of a more just society. This is an endeavor worth pursuing!

References

Chang, J., & Gaete, J. (2014). IPS supervision as relationally responsive practice. In K. Tomm, S. St. George, D. Wulff, & T. Strong (Eds.), *Patterns in interpersonal interactions: Inviting relational understandings for therapeutic change* (pp. 187–209). New York, NY: Routledge.

Greene, B. (2005). Psychology, diversity and social justice: Beyond heterosexism and across the cultural divide. *Counselling Psychology Quarterly, 18*(4), 295–306.

Hair, H. J. (2014). Supervision conversations about social justice and social work practice. *Journal of Social Work, 15*(4), 349–370.

Harrist, S., & Richardson, F. C. (2012). Disguised ideologies in counseling and social justice work. *Counseling and Values, 57*, 38–44.

Helms, J. E. (2003). A pragmatic view of social justice. *The Counseling Psychologist, 31*(3), 305–313. doi:10.1177/0010000325319

Ivey, A. E., & Collins, N. M. (2003). Social justice: A long-term challenge for counseling psychology. *The Counseling Psychologist, 31*(3), 290–298.

Kakkad, D. (2005). A new ethical praxis: Psychologists' emerging responsibilities in issues of social justice. *Ethics and Behavior, 15*(4), 293–308.

Kvale, S., & Brinkmann, S. (2009). *Interviews: Learning the craft of qualitative research interviewing* (2nd ed.). Thousand Oaks, CA: Sage.

Lock, A., & Strong, T. (2010). *Social constructionism: Sources and stirrings in theory and practice*. New York, NY: Cambridge University Press.

McLaughlin, A. M. (2009). Clinical social workers: Advocates for social justice. *Advances in Social Work, 10*(1), 51–68.

McLaughlin, A. M. (2011). Exploring social justice for clinical social work practice. *Smith College Studies in Social Work, 81*(2–3), 234–251. doi:10.1080/00377317.2011.588551

Paré, D. (2014). Social justice and the word: Keeping diversity alive in therapeutic conversations. *Canadian Journal of Counselling and Psychotherapy, 48*(3), 206–217.

Paré, D., Audet, C., Bailey, J., Caputo, A., Hatch, K., & Wong-Wylie, G. (2004). Courageous practice: Tales from reflexive supervision. *Canadian Journal of Counselling and Psychotherapy, 38*(2), 118–129.

Reason, P. (1998). Three approaches to participative inquiry. In N. K. Denzin & Y. S. Lincoln (Eds.), *Handbook of qualitative research* (pp. 324–339). Thousand Oaks, CA: Sage.

Rupani, P. (2013). Social justice and counselling psychology training: Can we learn from the US? *Counselling Psychology Review, 28*(2), 30–38.

Seedall, R. B., Holtrop, K., & Parra-Cardona, J. R. (2014). Diversity, social justice, and intersectionality trends in C/MFT: A content analysis of three family therapy journals, 2004–2011. *Journal of Marriage and Family Therapy, 40*(2), 139–151.

St. George, S., Wulff, D., & Strong, T. (2014). Researching interpersonal patterns. In K. Tomm, S. St. George, D. Wulff, & T. Strong (Eds.), *Patterns in interpersonal interactions: Inviting relational understandings for therapeutic change* (pp. 210–228). New York, NY: Routledge.

Strong, T. (2014). Conceptualizing interactional patterns: Theoretical threads to facilitate recognizing and responding to IPs. In K. Tomm, S. St. George, D. Wulff, & T. Strong (Eds.), *Patterns in interpersonal interactions: Inviting relational understandings for therapeutic change* (pp. 36–56). New York, NY: Routledge.

Thomas, F. (2003). And justice for all: Social justice in MFT training programs. *Family Therapy Magazine, 2*(1), 34–36. Retrieved from http://www.aamft.org/members/familytherapyresources/articles/ftm1v22003_34_36.htm

Tomm, K. (2014). Continuing the journey. In K. Tomm, S. St. George, D. Wulff, & T. Strong (Eds.), *Patterns in interpersonal interactions: Inviting relational understandings for therapeutic change* (pp. 229–247). New York, NY: Routledge.

Vallejos-Bartlett, C. (2003). In search of social justice: Thoughts from the field of family therapy. *Family Therapy Magazine, 2*(1), 16–23.

Chapter 6
Everyday Solution-Focused Recursion: When Family Therapy Faculty, Supervisors, Researchers, Students, and Clients Play Well Together

Ron Chenail, Arlene Brett Gordon, Jenna Wilson and Lori Pantaleao

Introduction

In academic clinical programs, a constant challenge is to transform the "hardening of the categories," that is, relational patterns keeping teachers, supervisors, researchers, students, and clients in traditional roles that support isolation, conflict, and disengagement. As with most educational organizations, we in our Department of Family Therapy (DFT) at Nova Southeastern University (NSU) in Fort Lauderdale, Florida, historically followed this pattern dutifully carrying out our work well within our faculty, administration, and student identities. We did so because that was the way we were taught and we certainly had success in doing so too. At the same time, we realized our clear-cut boundaries limited our creativity and perhaps our effectiveness. Maybe when you teach too much as a faculty member, you forget how to learn. Maybe if you learn all the time as a student, you do not learn how to teach. Possibly if you only practice therapy, you never gain an appreciation for research and if you only conduct clinical research, you may never advance as a therapist. What a shame this would be.

Maybe the central irony with how we were living as faculty and students was that we as family therapists were operating from a systemic, relational solution-focused perspective, but in our academia lifestyles, we were living more individualized, intrapersonal problem-focused lives fixating on our curriculum vitae, degree plans, and caseloads. Even though we found ourselves swimming daily in a school of people, our constructed demarcations between student and professor, clinician and researcher, and client and therapist resulted in us living on our own self-created and self-perpetuating personal islands.

As we began to recognize this tragic separation, we also began to consider a possible solution: Could we embrace a more mutually beneficial interpersonal

R. Chenail (✉) · A.B. Gordon · J. Wilson · L. Pantaleao
College of Arts, Humanities and Social Sciences, Nova Southeastern University, Fort Lauderdale, FL, USA
e-mail: ron@nova.edu

S. St. George and D. Wulff (eds.), *Family Therapy as Socially Transformative Practice*, AFTA SpringerBriefs in Family Therapy,
DOI 10.1007/978-3-319-29188-8_6

pattern of interacting with each other so we could bring out more in each other than the limited relationships we were invoking in our traditional courses, classes, and cases? Could some of our traditional ways of approaching education and learning be hindering how we co-constructed knowledge with each other especially when it comes to the faculty–student relationship? Could taking a pedagogical posture, that is, working from a stance of adult teachers treating adult students as children, lead us to unintentionally oppress adult graduate students and actually disable their learning as well as our own (Friere 1970)? As we became more and more aware of our participation in this type of hierarchical relationship, we began to ask ourselves new questions: Could we as faculty embrace a more andragogical perspective (Knowles 1984) and recognize graduate students as adults like ourselves, and appreciate what they can teach us (Cooperrider and Whitney 2005)? Could we take this appreciative inquiry stance with our students and ourselves a step further? Could we all learn to design our destinies by discovering our dreams (Cooperrider and Whitney 2005)? If successful, we could all find liberation from the traditional teacher–student relationship by flattening the hierarchy (Friere 1970), embracing an appreciative andragogy, and proceeding as co-learners.

Our response to this opportunity to address an oppressive power/knowledge relationship was to turn to our inner therapists and embrace a solution-focused recursion between the roles we play to "soften" traditional boundaries creating more playful, flat, relational patterns leading to more therapy-informed research, more research-informed clinical practices, and more egalitarian faculty–student relations. Oh, and the clients seem to benefit too in this transformational, appreciative process!

Embracing solution-focused brief therapy (SFBT) assumptions (Bavelas et al. 2013) was critical to our transformational practices. Holding these positive perspectives enabled us to stay focused on strengths, resources, and hopefulness as we worked toward developing new relational patterns with our department and clinic colleagues, peers, and clients. First and foremost, we based our actions on being solution-building rather than problem-solving. To us this meant we endeavored to seek out positive exceptions to the traditional relationships between teacher and student, between clinical practitioner and clinical researcher, and between client and therapist. We did not see any of these typical relations as being problematic, but rather envisioned them as opportunities for us to increase the frequency of useful behaviors and to discover new, valuable alternatives. We concentrated on the desired futures of ourselves and those with whom we interacted: What useful things did clients, students, and faculty want in their lives, what strengths and resources of theirs and ours could be amplified, and what small positive exceptions could be fostered into larger constructive increments of change? Lastly, we wanted to co-create these alternatives with all members of our department and clinics. This solution-focused quest was not to be an exertion by individuals but rather an effort of a collective community to transform itself for the betterment of all. Having said that, it is vital to remember another extremely important SFBT assumption: From little things big things come. For us, this meant solution-focused practice may start with one or two individuals utilizing strengths and resources to usher in change, but over time and through personal commitment these initial small successes beget more universal success, especially when progress is shared until transformative change eventually becomes the norm and not the exception.

Our first solution-focused step toward changing the way we interacted with each other was to soften our clearly defined academic and clinical identities in order to appreciate how much more we were similar to each other than different. Professors, researchers, students, and clients are all interested in learning. We seek valuable insights from our scholarship, research, and personal explorations. We reflect on these lessons and hopefully, become wiser in the process. We may employ different methods, operate from different theoretical perspectives, and use different media to make our findings public, but in the end, we are all trying to discover new knowledge and make our lives better. Recognizing these similarities enabled us to collaborate in ways we would never have done if we kept to our traditional divides. Regardless of our "official" roles, we all could teach, we all could learn, and we all could change. The simple recursions of seeing therapists helping clients to change and clients as change agents for therapists, researchers producing therapeutic results and therapists generating significant findings, and students professing lessons learned and professors learning students' insights helped us to transform the ways we teach, learn, research, treat, train, and grow.

We operationalized our solution-focused approach to transforming our relationships by using five common SFBT practices: (a) co-create with experts, (b) focus on other's focus, (c) lead from behind, (d) look for what's better, and (e) co-measure progress. Co-creating with experts helped us to keep our relationships non-hierarchical, respectful, and curious. As teachers we sought our students' knowledge, as therapists we respected the strengths of our clients, and we transformed collaboratively. Focusing on other's focus helped us to appreciate what was valuable to the others with whom we worked. For example, knowing students' career paths helped us as professors and supervisors to co-construct learning activities that not only helped the students to demonstrate learning competencies, but also to produce real-world products such as publications based upon in-class assignments which helped them to develop competitive portfolios for their own faculty positions. Putting their goals and aspirations firmly in focus helped us all to co-create transformative experiences beneficial to all parties involved. This focus on focus made it easy for us to then lead from behind because we all had agreed on the directions we were taking together. For instance, with the in-class papers, we could help students select prospective publication outlets, provide feedback in line with the guidance they would receive from an editorial board, and then provide consultation throughout the editorial process. Throughout the transformative process, we consistently looked for what was better in any aspect of our interactions, products, and outcomes. For the writing projects, we would note strengths in the papers and encourage more and better sections. No matter how small an improvement was, we honored that accomplishment and shared the success widely (i.e., asking students to present exemplary writing excerpts to their classmates), so we helped to cultivate little successes into bigger and more frequent ones. Throughout the transformative process, we endeavored to co-measure progress, so everyone had a voice in recognizing growth, advancement, and development. With students' papers, we might ask them to make the first assessment using a rubric evaluating quality on a scale of 1–10 and then talk with them about the strengths they saw as well as what we observed as positives and then co-construct a revision strategy for the next draft. For each draft, we would note the development of the paper's quality until we reached our co-agreed goal, maybe an 8 out of 10 or better. In doing so, teacher and student both learned how to become experts about the paper's quality, building on better drafts celebrating progress toward not only writing a great paper, but also maybe eventually crafting a published article helping the student take a big step toward an ultimate career goal in the academy.

In this chapter, as co-authors we share our collective and individual solution-focused stories of how we have begun to learn how to learn as part of a vibrant, solution-focused transformative community that our department and clinic have become. In doing so we also model the meaningful recursive solution-focused relationships, we have grown to embrace in our day-to-day practice of working and learning together.

As we progress in our careers, we will continue to embrace this recursive solution-focused learning life-style. If we are successful with this pursuit, we will help to transform the new communities within which we will work and play. We have already seen evidence of this transformative effect in our own department, clinic, and college; and as we continue to write, present, teach, treat, supervise, and research, we hope to influence the people, communities, and organizations we encounter, and to learn more about ourselves in the process.

So, as you read this chapter, we encourage you to embrace these simple solution-focused practices: see yourself as experts seeking out other experts with whom you will co-create transformative practices; learn to learn the desired futures of others focusing on what is and what could be better; collaborate by leading from behind treasuring even the smallest positive exceptions, strengths, and resources and amplify their intensity, frequency, and appreciation; and co-measure your progress together and co-celebrate the transformations. Lastly, we ask you to embrace this everyday solution-focused recursion by remembering to "soften the categories" so you, too, build mutually beneficial relationships with other co-experts leading to better transformative practices.

Ron's Story: From Clinical Researchers to Researching Clinicians

For many years as a professor of family therapy, I have taught the two qualitative research courses in our PhD in family therapy program. Our students take these classes at the end of their second year in their studies as they are completing their internal practicums and beginning to undertake their external internships. They are also embarking on their portfolio capstones, clinical and research, in which they demonstrate their competencies in these areas. Upon completion of their capstones, the students can officially begin their dissertation process by selecting a chair, committee, and topic.

Over the past decade or so, I found the students to be more and more stressed mostly due to their co-curricular demands, namely the capstones (Chenail 2004). In the clinical capstone, they present their model of therapy via a paper and case presentation, and in the research capstone, they report on a research project they have conducted. Both of these capstones were typically done during the winter and summer semesters in which I taught the qualitative research classes.

I certainly was sensitive to the students' anxiety over their capstones, but I was also sensitive to my role in preparing them to conceive, conduct, and report on their dissertation research. To this end, I would introduce the students to qualitative research and its applications to clinical research. With the support and encouragement of Arlene Gordon, Director of the Brief Therapy Institute (BTI), our department's clinic, they would work in teams to conduct actual qualitative research studies from BTI data and write up their results. We ended up producing a series of national presentations and publications (e.g., Chenail et al. 2009; Heller et al. 2010; Somers et al. 2010) and our work on how students composed their progress notes led to a series of improvements in how we taught and structured case documentation in our clinic. Together as experts, we were co-constructing new clinical procedures, products, and practices helping to transform our program.

Despite the publications, presentations, and the transformative enhancements to our clinic's policies and procedures, I was still concerned about the students' stress balancing the demands of the two qualitative research classes, their capstones, external internships, and dissertations. I was also cognizant of the career pathways most of our doctoral students took. For the vast majority of our graduates, their careers were dominated by clinical work. Many went into clinical practice solely, some combined this work with part-time teaching and supervision, and fewer took full-time faculty positions. Even those who became professors tended to take positions dominated by teaching and clinical supervision. All of these graduates would use research to help inform their clinical work, but they were for the most part not becoming researchers. This insight helped me finally to get a better sense of the students' focus.

This solution-focused outcome assessment caused me to reflect upon what and how I was teaching and to begin to focus more on who I was teaching—reflective clinicians (Chenail 2013). My students loved clinical work and their career choices reflected this affinity to therapy and supervision. This "A-Ha" moment helped me to see that I had been working hard to create clinical researchers instead of helping my students become better researching clinicians (see Wulff and St. George, Researcher as Practitioner: Practitioner as Researcher 2016). This perspective allowed me to begin to lead these expert clinicians from behind because I could see where they wanted to go career-wise.

With this solution-focused epiphany in mind, I redesigned the two qualitative research courses to show students how they could use research to become better clinicians. I simplified the array of methodologies I taught to primarily focus on case study (Creswell 2012) which is the foundation of clinical work as well as clinical research—we always start with a case whether we are therapists, supervisors, or researchers conducting an "N of 1" design or a large-scale controlled study. As for the assignments, I had students study a famous SFBT (Berg 2004) case conducted by Insoo Kim Berg, SFBT co-founder, and produce a paper in which they explored some aspect of the clinical processes they observed in the case. In doing so, the students could show their qualitative research competencies while experiencing an in-depth study of a therapeutic approach many of them would use widely in their clinical practice and teaching.

In working with the students on their case studies, I broke assignments down into small pieces, so one week the students might work solely on the introduction. They only had to write a short piece and I only had to give feedback on a small piece. I would focus on the positives in the writing; always letting the students know that their papers are not just written, but rewritten and rewritten. This helped them to appreciate the writing process as they could see the improvements section by section. I would co-present exemplary papers with students in class and online, so we could share writing insights encouraging others to embrace a central solution-focused tenet of trying "what works" for themselves.

The transformative impact of the researching process on the students' clinical know-how was immediate. They reported the use of the qualitative case study methods helped them to appreciate SFBT like they never had done so before. They also shared that their qualitative analysis of the case helped them to practice SFBT more effectively and more as the "pragmatics of hope and respect" (Berg and Dolan 2001, p. 1) as SFBT was originally designed.

As an added bonus, the students' in-class work helped them to complete their two capstones. The students learned how to study a case using a variety of qualitative methodologies helping them to improve their clinical portfolio case study papers and presentations. In addition, they submitted revised case study research papers for their research portfolios. The successes of the first group of students using this strategy of leveraging their coursework to navigate the capstones gave subsequent students the confidence they, too, could multitask their way through the challenges of their research courses and capstones. Success was leading to more success!

A number of these students also used their in-class research projects to create conference presentations they have made and papers they are now submitting to journals for publication. Their case studies are also serving as the foundations of their dissertations. So, even though I changed the classes to help the students become better clinicians, they have also shown the ability to become accomplished researchers along the way—a delightful solution-focused recursion indeed.

Arlene's Story: Permeable Boundaries in Solution-Focused Supervision

From a solution-focused perspective, therapeutic and supervisory activities are isomorphic throughout the entire system. This parallel recursive process is intrinsic to the relationship between teacher–student, supervisor–supervisee, and its consistency provides a more clear and reliable theoretical foundation for supervision.

Solution-focused supervision is also a collaborative process in which both the supervisee and the supervisor share their ideas and learn from each other (Messmore et al. 2014).

I became a solution-focused therapist almost 25 years ago as a doctoral student studying marriage and family therapy (MFT) at Nova Southeastern University. During my third practicum, my clinical supervisor was Dr. Lee Shilts, a well-known solution-focused therapist (see Berg and Shilts 2004). Lee studied and worked with SFBT co-founders, Insoo Kim Berg and Steve de Shazer. Lee's practice and his supervision were interactive translations of SFBT principles. During therapy sessions, clients were consistently engaged by his collaborative spirit inviting them, as experts in their own lives (see also Ashbourne et al. Supporting the Development of Novice Therapists 2016), to envision a future when the problem that brought them to therapy was no longer a problem. It was not unusual for clients to report positive change after their initial session.

As a practicum supervisor, Lee's solution-focused supervision was as engaging as his therapy. He invited practicum team members to maintain a solution-focused, collaborative, reflective posture systemically in relation to the client, each other, and the supervisor. He established a context for curiosity, seeking an evolution of solution-focused ideas specific to each session. Lee's non-directive posture encouraged us to focus on what clients, as experts, wanted from each session.

Lee concentrated on our understanding of the recursive nature of solution-focused practice through his solution-focused supervision. His collaborative posture blurred the boundaries between teacher/student and between supervisor/supervisee. He actively invited students as co-authors and co-presenters, supporting our work in the family therapy community. Before my graduation, Lee and I published two articles together (Shilts and Gordon 1993, 1996) on the miracle question based on our clinical experiences. Together we presented at conferences as colleagues. And Lee had another gift to share with me.

I met Insoo Kim Berg and Steve de Shazer in 1991 during one of our practicum classes. Insoo sat next to me in front of the one-way mirror as our team was watching a family session. She inched up close to the mirror as not to miss a detail. I heard her exclaimed "wows" as she highlighted what the therapist was doing well and complimenting the family's efforts. She expressed her curiosity about what might be useful to the family and worked with us to focus on our understanding of what was important from the family's perspective. We incorporated solution-focused questions to ask our clients and to ask ourselves in relation to our clients.

During session breaks, Insoo's supportive supervision focused more on the client rather than the therapist. The clients, the student therapist, the team members were all customers for change. She guided us by "leading from one step behind," establishing a mentoring relationship based on mutual respect, collaboration, and a sharing of knowledge to create a culture for positive change (De Jong and Berg 2008). The focus was on solution-building rather than problem-solving skills for both clients and students. Insoo's supervision questions were parallel to the questions we asked our clients: "*What do you think might be the first step?*" "*What will the family be doing that will let you know that they are moving towards their miracle?*" Together the team co-created a shared vision.

We had clients scale their progress. We scaled ours.

Early during my work with Lee, I found SFBT a natural fit for who I was and how I understood the world (Shilts and Gordon 1996). And now I was getting the opportunity to work directly with Insoo Kim Berg, who loved Florida's weather. Insoo would visit biannually to work with Lee and students at NSU. Fortunately for me, I was invited to the majority of those visits.

During that time, SFBT (de Shazer 1985) was in its early development. Insoo relished coming to a university with faculty and students who embraced their work. For years, she would conduct workshops and provide practicum supervision at our clinic. Her supervision was isomorphic to her therapy, her mentoring, and to her way of being. She invited both students and faculty to work with her on writing about what they were learning from their individual, yet collaborative, perspectives (Rudes et al. 1997).

After graduation, I continued to adhere to the basic principles of SFBT as adjunct faculty/practicum supervisor. I embraced a "not-knowing stance," which enabled me to listen to and learn more from my clients and my students. I incorporated solution-focused questions into our practicum conversations (Braus et al. 2003). Together we explored exceptions, noticing small change that may lead to larger change.

Currently, I am the director of the BTI at Nova Southeastern University's College of Arts, Humanities, and Social Sciences. Our family therapy clinic is the training site for master's and doctoral students in the DFT. In addition to providing students with clinical training, the BTI sponsors ongoing educational activities to support our students' growth as well-rounded practitioners, teachers, and researchers. For example, BTI sponsors free ongoing workshops for our students. Topics are determined by the presenters which often are collaborations between a faculty member and students. Recent monthly topics have presented the activities of individual faculty members such as equine therapy, relational suicide assessment (Flemons and Gralnick 2013), and working with veterans. Topics typically help students grasp new therapeutic applications and techniques.

To reach a wider audience, together with my co-architect, Dr. Jenna Wilson, at the time a family therapy doctoral student and now a graduate of the PhD program, we began developing a SFBT Webcast series with the support of NSU's Office of Innovation and Information Technology and support personnel. The series includes a wide range of applications of SFBT in diverse settings. Our goal was to create a virtual classroom experience. Topics include SFBT 101, advanced skill building, hope-focused solutions, and working with children and adolescents, to name a few. By "softening the categories" between teacher and student, Jenna and I were able to co-create a fascinating array of products. To continue to reach interested practitioners, we decided to create a SFBT Library of the Webcasts which provides access to the trainings after they streamed live. The SFBT Webcast Library is currently located at http://cahss.nova.edu/familytherapywebinar/index.html. As the program continues to develop, new PhD students have joined the team to sustain the recursive relationship between teacher and students teaching new students.

I also am a solution-focused supervisor for practica and independent doctoral students working at the Family Therapy Clinic at BTI. From my perspective, solution-focused supervision is a self-reflective practice. As a therapist, I ask myself questions about what I am doing well and what do I need to do better. I consider my miracle for each case. I scale my understanding of our progress. As a supervisor in this isomorphic process, I ask my supervisees the same reflective questions. Our focus is on highlighting the supervisee's competencies and exploring new skills that need to develop.

Over the years, I continue to consult, train, and present with my long-time colleague, Dr. Carol Messmore, Program Director at Capella University. Carol is a solution-focused therapist with a very similar training background as mine, working with both Insoo Kim Berg and Lee Shilts. In addition, Carol was a practicum supervisor at NSU over the years. Today, Carol and I meet to share ideas and reflections about teaching and supervising students learning SFBT. We discuss our challenges and continue to navigate utilizing solution-focused practices.

Carol and I mentor the students we work with isomorphically to the way we were mentored. We are curious about our students' interests, which leads us into conversations about next steps. We encourage students to work with us on projects and presentations. Together with our students, we present at national conferences and co-author trainings. For example, last year Carol and I presented with a doctoral student, Michael Rolleston, on the multilayers of SFBT supervision. The first part of our presentation included video clips of supervision sessions to demonstrate the recursive nature of solution-focused supervision. These were followed up by clips of conversations between the supervisees about their experiences. The videos included clips of the conversations between supervisees and supervisors utilizing a tapestry of SFBT strategies. As supervisors collaborating with our supervisees, we sought, respectfully, to contextualize these sessions as conversations rather than one-on-one lectures. We share clips of supervision and discuss their experiences with SFBT supervision at BTI. Currently, Carol and I continue to explore the permeable boundaries of solution-focused supervision.

Several years ago, Dr. Ron Chenail, professor of family therapy, redesigned the program's qualitative research course to invite students to explore clinical applications from a researcher's perspective. As the students focused more on videos of Insoo Kim Berg's solution-focused strategies with the clients, students began to look at their clinical work as research.

A new generation of students researching SFBT under the guidance of Ron are embracing a solution-focused posture in their clinical work and applying concepts they explored in qualitative research class into their clinical practice. Their research is informing their therapy and their therapy is informing their research and project development. All grow more skillful in their area of focus, teaching their teachers through their process. They demonstrate, in their own ways, weaving research and clinical experience. Students have taken interventions from practicum experience, woven in what they learned in Ron's qualitative research classes and apply those learnings in dissertations and projects. Ron's research has stimulated greater interest and understanding of the solution-focused model.

Many of those students interested in exploring SFBT practices beyond the classroom worked with me in BTI. Two of these colleagues are collaborators in this chapter. During her dissertation process, Jenna Wilson, with mentoring by Ron Chenail, incorporated the role of hope within solution-focused therapy. Lori Pantelano's dissertation training project emerged from a family therapy session during a practicum.

Students' therapy experiences grew into research projects and evolved into resources to share with other practitioners. The recursive process regenerates. One example is provided by Michael Rolleston, a current doctoral student working as a graduate assistant in the BTI. Over a brief period of time, Michael realized that a majority of his cases focused on adolescent young men dealing with life-changing challenges. He explored different ways to ask the miracle question so that it would be more specific to each case. During our supervision, we discussed different ways to phrase the miracle question. Michael grew more curious about these ideas and worked on them in his qualitative research classes with Ron and is now researching the use of the miracle question with diverse of populations for his dissertation.

Another doctoral student, Laquana Young, is working with Ron on her applied clinical project. She, too, is focusing on hope as a result of her clinical experiences at BTI. During our practicum, and as an independent doctoral therapist in the clinic, Laquana used art work to incorporate solution-focused metaphors with children.

Solution-focused attention transcends the boundaries of the therapy room. It makes boundaries permeable between individuals, particularly between individuals in traditionally defined hierarchies such as professor/student, supervisor/supervisee, mentor/mentee, and therapist/client. This model opens the boundaries between those roles. Because solution-focused work attends to connections that are beneficial for individuals in their relationships with each other, these relationships evolve into professor:student, supervisor:supervisee, mentor:mentee, and therapist:client. These relationships, sustained with a solution-focused lens, allow for miracles through natural connections.

Jenna's Story: Experiencing the Recursive Nature of Being a Lifelong Learner

In May of 2015, I defended my dissertation and in June I graduated with my PhD in MFT from Nova Southeastern University. I began my master's degree in MFT in 2009. I had just finished my undergraduate studies in psychology with a minor in sociology. Just before that, I was fresh out of high school and eager to explore what it meant to be a college student. I had always loved learning and appreciated the power of knowledge.

Upon reflection, I am able to experience and appreciate all of the various roles I have played throughout my academic career as a student, clinician, researcher, supervisor, trainer, presenter, author, and now a faculty member. I am currently an adjunct faculty teaching doctoral students in Nova's College of Arts, Humanities, and Social Sciences (CAHSS), DFT, and in Nova's College of Psychology.

It is now easy for me to articulate how the collaborative, solution-focused stance of our program and clinic has allowed me to develop both personally and professionally. The categories were "softened" in such a way that while I was a student, I also had the opportunity to teach a lecture alongside my professor as a teaching assistant. While I was working toward licensure in MFT as a registered intern, I was able to practice being a supervisor through opportunities in the BTI as a supervisor assistant as well as a practicing clinician under supervision. My professors and supervisors encouraged me to take advantage of these opportunities demonstrating the SFBT idea of co-construction and collaboration.

In the doctoral program, I first noted the recursive nature of my experience as an observer to the observed. I was able to reflect on the process of my process, which in the Master's program I was trained to do not only as a clinician with my clients but also as a developing faculty and researcher as I advanced my studies in the doctoral program. Holding true to the SFBT notion of collaborating with others based on strengths as well as taking the one-down stance, Dr. Tommie Boyd approached me with my first opportunity to present at the American Association of Marriage and Family Therapy (AAMFT) national conference the year I began my doctoral studies (Boyd et al. 2012). This was my first doctoral experience in balancing multiple roles and the "softening" of rigid boundaries and hierarchy for professionals. I was still a student but was also given the opportunity to present alongside my professor, who also happened to be the department chair. I could see how Dr. Boyd led me from one step behind and allowed me to take the initiative on the presentation while also guiding and nudging me gently in a useful direction because she also understood this was my first conference presentation. In SFBT, we nudge and lead our clients and supervisees toward their goals, strengths, and resources in a very similar way.

I have since done multiple presentations and trainings at professional conferences nationally and internationally. I was developing various systemic understandings of the world and the more I developed my systemic ideas, the more I was able to teach them to others. I then began noticing the more opportunities I was given to teach these systemic ideas to others, the more I was learning, developing, and refining my systemic understandings of the world. This process is similar to the relational piece of SFBT in which circularity and recursiveness are useful.

For me, this "softened" the "hardening of the categories" and allowed me to observe how I am, and always will be, a lifelong learner. The professional playfulness opened up so many possibilities that could have been limited due to rigid relational boundaries. From time to time, I had multiple conversations with Arlene Gordon and became her supervisor assistant/candidate in clinical practica. In addition, I was invited to co-create a webinar series with Arlene on hope-focused solutions. This webinar series was the first in the department, so it also was a significant learning curve for the both of us. We continuously co-measured our progress and focused on our desired future.

Arlene's sharing of her vast amount of knowledge in SFBT and her personal and professional stories about studying alongside Insoo Kim Berg inspired me to push my own professional boundaries in a way that encouraged and supported creativity, exploration, and possibility. I also became involved in the process of writing and submitting research grants as well as conducting qualitative process research. The family therapy program felt like a family, encouraging growth, hope, possibility, and success not only for students, but also for faculty and clients alike.

Until I took my first qualitative research course in the MFT doctoral program, I had thought of myself as a student, clinician, and aspiring faculty and supervisor. I was apprehensive about research. The title "researcher" seemed so intimidating. What did it mean to be a researcher? In this course, I learned how I could utilize research to enhance my clinical understanding with my clients and also learned how this enhanced clinical understanding could influence my role as a researcher. Ron Chenail asked the class to choose an area of interest in the SFBT model to study and analyze. Some classmates chose the miracle question, others chose exploring exceptions and the patterns thereof. I chose the role of hope since I was curious to understand how Insoo Kim Berg built hope with her clients.

I had a basic content-level understanding of SFBT from my master's study, but now I was eager to understand the role of hope in SFBT by examining how Berg seemingly built hope with her clients relationally. Berg and Dolan (2001) described the essence of SFBT as the "pragmatics of hope and respect" (p. 1). Despite the declaration of the importance of hope in SFBT, I saw little process research looking at the "pragmatics" of hope in SFBT clinical practice. This was a gap in the research and my opportunity to conduct a meaningful research project.

It was this curiosity and encouragement to get playful with these ideas that allowed me to use the two qualitative research doctoral courses to analyze a case study by Berg (2004) in such a way that I developed a preliminary theory of how Insoo Kim Berg built hope with clients. Through my role as researcher, I acquired a new appreciation and understanding of SFBT.

Not only did the discovery of this relational pattern of building hope serve as my research capstone, but it also became the foundation for my dissertation. I was no longer intimidated by the researcher title and was able to consider myself a qualitative researcher. Again, it was this "softening of the categories" that allowed me to become curious enough about research that I could be playful with the ideas long enough to develop them into meaningful and professional pieces of work. I explored these hope-filled ideas endlessly. I continue to learn more about the role of hope not only in SFBT but in all schools of therapy.

The title of my dissertation is *Hope-Focused Solutions: A Relational Hope Focus of the Solution-Building Stages in SFBT* (Wilson 2015). My dissertation, chaired by Ron Chenail, focused on analyzing three cases by Insoo Kim Berg utilizing grounded theory (Charmaz 2014) to attend to how Berg listened, selected, and built hope relationally with clients to validate her progression within and across the five solution-building stages of SFBT. My findings were congruent with the basic tenets of SFBT and I was able to make the pragmatics of hope and respect more transparent for future practitioners of SFBT.

I continue my researching therapist journey with these ideas and have begun to share them with a larger clinical community (e.g., Wilson et al. 2015) with the opportunity to learn more about these ideas as I expand my conversation with colleagues worldwide. The playful SFBT recursions and "softening" of the categories inside our clinical program and now beyond, these ongoing experiences have had a significant and meaningful influence on my personal journey and professional career.

Lori's Story: Family Therapy as Socially Transformative Practice—Practical Strategies

In 2010, I started as a student in a MFT doctoral program. Now at this point in my career, I have been in higher education longer than the mandatory 12 years of parochial school. My family, friends, and even professors have referred me to as "the professional student." However the collaborative, co-creative solution-focused approach to teaching and developing relationships between faculty and students that I experienced at NSU moved me to consider myself a "professional learner."

I entered the MFT field with a theoretical stance that was shaken by experiencing solution-focused live supervision. In addition, I was initially apprehensive about being observed, having suggestions called in, and taking a break mid-session for feedback. In my first practicum session with a family, my anxiety was high.

The family[1] came into the BTI with an "anxious" adolescent. In the first two sessions, mom and dad expressed their concerns about their son and daughter and their goal of coming into therapy to "fix their children." The son would not speak at all in session. By examining and reflecting upon my personal assumptions in supervision, I was able to develop ways to build a collaborative therapeutic relationship with the adolescent son. I believed the only way this young man would share his story with me was for me to put myself in his shoes, and so I did, literally. I had the same pair of shoes as the client and I wore them to the second session hoping to "soften the categories" between us. I concentrated on leading the session from behind by focusing on the son's expertise which also helped to "soften" the traditional client/therapist roles.

With the assistance of solution-focused supervision, my curiosity about this client grew. I learned that he was a fan of the Miami's professional basketball team. I was able to incorporate the client's interest in this basketball team to co-construct a unique progress scale that he would use to rate his level of anxiety. I have found that when working with adolescents, "a scale with simple numbers may not fully hold their attention or assist in comprehending the question. Using a metaphor that emphasizes their interests encourages engagement and produces a working knowledge of the ratings on the scale" (Pantaleao and Rambo 2014, p. 21). The client and I

[1]We have changed identifying information for all clients mentioned in the chapter.

modified this well-known SFBT scaling technique to fit our therapeutic needs. The client needed a way to communicate and I needed a way to understand him. We would co-measure the client's progress through the metaphoric basketball scaling question. I was able to co-create with the client, focus on his focus of anxiety, lead the client from one step behind using his language, and look for what was better through the co-measurement of the basketball scaling question. Through this experience, I was motivated to develop a Metaphorically Enhanced Scaling Question (MESQ) and develop a training program which became the topic of my dissertation.

The next phase after completing all my coursework in the doctoral program was to create a series of portfolios. My supervisor, "leading from one step behind," encouraged me to integrate my clinical experience in the portfolios and I used the basketball scaling experience as a grounding for those portfolios and my subsequent dissertation. In hindsight, the development of the MESQ training program is an example of a recursive process.

Currently, I am in the teacher and learner phase of this cycle as I am teaching the MESQ technique to novice and seasoned therapists, learning something new each time I teach. My professional development is an illustration of the recursion cycle from student, to author, to researcher, to teacher, to therapist, and back to student again.

Reflections

As we composed and read our individual sections for this chapter we were struck by the similarities our experiences reflect. We enjoy working with each other, we learn and share what we learn with ourselves and others, and we flow gracefully among clinician, researcher, and educator identities on a life-long learning plane. At the same time, as we soften these categories, each of these identities becomes transformed as we bring research lessons to the clinic, clinical wisdom to the research laboratory, and clinical research practice and research insights to our teaching and supervision. We also embrace a solution-focused posture in our professional and personal relationships which keeps us curious, respectful, and hopeful as we strive to improve our practices. Lastly with this appreciative inquiry, we continue to discover new dreams helping us to design new destinies for ourselves and the communities in which we live and learn.

References

Bavelas, J., De Jong, P., Franklin, C., Froerer, A., Gingerich, W., Kim, J., et al. (2013). *Solution focused therapy treatment manual for working with individuals* (2nd ed.). Santa Fe, NM: Solution Focused Brief Therapy Association. Retrieved from http://sfbta.org/PDFs/researchDownloads/fileDownloader.asp?fname=SFBT_Revised_Treatment_Manual_2013.pdf

Berg, I. K. (2004). *Irreconcilable differences: A solution-focused approach to marital therapy* (Video file). Retrieved from http://ctiv.alexanderstreet.com.ezproxylocal.library.nova.edu/view/1778954

Berg, I. K., & Dolan, Y. (2001). *Tales of solutions: A collection of hope-inspiring stories*. New York, NY: W. W. Norton.

Berg, I. K., & Shilts, L. (2004). *Classroom solutions: Woww approach*. Milwaukee, WI: BFTC Press.

Boyd, T., Wilson, J., & Giraldez, D. (2012). *So your client is attracted to you?... now what?* (PowerPoint slides). Workshop presented at The American Association for Marriage and Family Therapy Conference (AAMFT), Charlotte, NC.

Braus, S., Cole, J., Reilly, S., Scieszinski, P., & Surowiec, S. (2003). *Supervision and mentoring in child welfare services*. Retrieved from http://www.sfbta.org/trainingLinks.html

Charmaz, K. (2014). *Constructing grounded theory* (2nd ed.). Los Angeles, CA: Sage.

Chenail, R. (2004). Commentary on tracking and revisiting the evolving perspective of an intern. *Journal of Systemic Therapies, 23*(3), 19–20.

Chenail, R. J. (2013). Forward: Becoming competent with competencies or what I have learned about learning. In D. Gehart (Ed.), *Mastering competencies in family therapy: A practical approach to theory and clinical case documentation* (2nd ed., pp. xxvii–xxix). Florence, KY: Cengage Learning.

Chenail, R. J., Somers, C. V., & Benjamin, J. D. (2009). A recursive frame qualitative analysis of MFT progress note tipping points. *Contemporary Family Therapy, 31*(2), 87–99. doi:10.1007/s10591-009-9085-7

Cooperrider, D. L., & Whitney, D. (2005). *Appreciative inquiry: A positive revolution in change*. San Francisco, CA: Berrett-Koehler Communications.

Creswell, J. (2012). *Qualitative inquiry and research design: Choosing among five approaches* (3rd ed.). Thousand Oaks, CA: Sage.

de Shazer, S. (1985). *Keys to solution in brief therapy*. New York, NY: Norton.

Flemons, D., & Gralnick, L. M. (2013). *Relational suicide assessment: Risks, resources, and possibilities for safety*. New York, NY: Norton.

Freire, P. (1970). *Pedagogy of the oppressed*. New York, NY: Continuum.

Heller, R. J., Gilliam, L. S., Chenail, R. J., & Hall, T. (2010). Three authors, one client: A qualitative description of marriage and family therapy initial case documentation. *Contemporary Family Therapy, 32*, 363–374. doi:10.1007/s10591-010-9130-6

Jong, P. D., & Berg, I. K. (2008). *Interviewing for solutions* (3rd ed.). Belmont: Thomson Brooks/Cole.

Knowles, M. (1984). *The adult learner: A neglected species* (3rd ed.). Houston, TX: Gulf.

Messmore, C., Gordon, A. B., & Rolleston, M. (2014). *Multiple layers of solution focused supervision: MFT training*. Workshop presented at Solution-Focused Brief Therapy Association: Santa Fe, NM.

Pantaleao, L., & Rambo, A. (2014). "Are you a LeBron today?" Playfully expanding scaling questions. *International Journal of Solution-Focused Practices, 2*(1), 20–23. doi:10.14335/ijsfp.v2i1.18

Rudes, J., Shilts, L., & Berg, I. K. (1997). Focused supervision seen through a recursive frame analysis. *Journal of Marital and Family Therapy, 23*, 203–215.

Shilts, L., & Gordon, A. B. (1993). Simplifying the miracle question. *Family Therapy Case Studies, 7*, 53–59.

Shilts, L., & Gordon, A. B. (1996). What to do after the miracle occurs. *Journal of Family Psychotherapy, 7*(1), 15–22.

Somers, C. V., Benjamin, J. D., & Chenail, R. J. (2010). How master's students document stability and change within and across progress notes. *Contemporary Family Therapy, 32*(1), 22–38. doi:10.1007/s10591-009-9105-7

Wilson, J. (2015). *Hope-focused solutions: A relational hope focus of the solution-building stages in solution-focused brief therapy (unpublished dissertation)*. Fort Lauderdale, FL: Nova Southeastern University.

Wilson, J., & Chenail, R. (2015). *Using utilization to build hope in solution-focused brief therapy* (PowerPoint Slides). Workshop presented at The 12th International Erickson Congress: Phoenix, AZ.

Chapter 7
Family Therapy Stories: Stretching Customary Family Therapy Practices

Sally St. George, Dan Wulff, Ron Chenail, Lynda J. Snyder, Lynda M. Ashbourne, Faye Gosnell and Shannon McIntosh

Introduction

Everyday injustices are not low-level experiences—they can be profound and life-altering. What follows are stories that point to the personal significance this topic has for each of the authors that serves to extend the chapters we have each written in this book entitled *Family Therapy as Socially Transformative Practice: Practical Strategies for Today and Tomorrow* (St. George and Wulff 2016). Our purpose in presenting these stories is to illustrate our most current collisions with social justice issues and possibilities about rectifying them through our daily work.

S. St. George (✉) · D. Wulff
Faculty of Social Work, University of Calgary, Calgary, AB, Canada
e-mail: sstgeor@ucalgary.ca

D. Wulff
e-mail: calgary_home@shaw.ca

R. Chenail
College of Arts, Humanities, and Social Sciences, Nova Southeastern University, Fort Lauderdale, FL, USA

L.J. Snyder
Calgary Family Therapy Centre, Calgary, AB, Canada

L.M. Ashbourne
Department of Family Relations and Applied Nutrition (Couple and Family Therapy), University of Guelph, Guelph, ON, Canada

F. Gosnell
Counselling Psychology, Calgary Family Therapy Centre, Calgary, AB, Canada

S. McIntosh
Alberta Health Services' Child & Adolescent Addictions & Mental Health, Specialized Services, Calgary, AB, Canada

S. St. George and D. Wulff (eds.), *Family Therapy as Socially Transformative Practice*, AFTA SpringerBriefs in Family Therapy,
DOI 10.1007/978-3-319-29188-8_7

It Happened Again…

By Sally

Our students are expected to attend to social justice issues in their practice of family therapy. Yet how to articulate what that is and how it is done, remains rather elusive. Sally tries by offering some questions to help her class discuss this noble yet difficult expectation.

It happened in class yesterday, yet again. A student said,

> We are supposed to see, hear, and talk social justice in our clinical work. But I do not think I am getting it. I think I know what social justice is, I can see it on a macro-level but in our clinical, one-on-one micro work I just do not think I can see it. Maybe others are way ahead of me and maybe all of you will think I am slow or incompetent, but I really do not think I can see it, hear it, and only talk about it in an educative, maybe theoretical way. Can we talk about what social justice is, one more time?

Before I could even form a word, there was a chorus of agreement and pleas for talking about what social justice in clinical work is.

This is not exactly an easy topic for me either and I think that I have more questions than I have answers. When that is the case, I, like many others, revert to stories. At the risk of repeating myself, I told them the story of the women in transitional housing (see St. George and Wulff, Family Therapy + Social Justice + Daily Practices = Transforming Therapy, 2016) who in our view did not feel entitled to treatment as worthy women deserving good jobs, respectful treatment in relationships, permanent relationships, opportunities to move out of their lower social class location, but most deserving of free holiday food and outraged when the local markets scaled back and decided not to donate holiday food to the residents in this housing program. I then gave them my interpretation that the injustice was less about not getting the food they expected, but more that they were in a position to not feel worthy or deserving of any of the things that many of us as women feel entitled to receive.

I admitted that I did not have a firm definition of social justice/injustice, but I could say that it has something to do with who is included, who is excluded, who is considered deserving, and who is not considered deserving. Then I developed questions for their consideration:

- *Where do you hear conversations that focus on including and/or excluding people?*
- *Where do you hear stories of entitlement, that is, who is allowed to have goods, opportunities, and privileges and who is not?*
- *Do you notice comments that give permission to others? Create expectations for others? Who seems to have the right to grant permission or set expectations for others?*
- *Do you recall times and places when you have been excluded and felt mistreated as a consequence?*
- *How can you protest these unfairnesses/injustices without further marginalizing yourself?*

Containing Emotions

By Lynda S.

Sometimes we get upset by the stories we are witness to, the stories that are accounts of the injustices that our clients experience, that they should not have to experience. I (Sally) often find myself saying to my students, "That anyone should have to suffer this is what is unjust." The sense of outrage or devastation that we can feel when we come close to our clients' stories poses a dilemma for us: Do we mask those feelings and create an air of calm and detachedness? If we let those feelings out, are we betraying our "professional stance?" Lynda S. walks us through supervisory interactions that address this issue to a place where emotions can help transform therapy and supervision.

She walked into my office and closed the door. "Do you have a minute?" she asked. Her eyes had that deer-in-the-headlights look and I set aside my clinical notes and invited her to have a chair. Silence dominated the room as she appeared to figuratively collect herself. "Whew, I just had quite a session…" and her eyes filled with tears.

The moment was poignant with opportunities for me to speak but I chose to be silent and provide her space to experience the impact of the session. In the quietness, she also made a decision to risk sharing her response to the disclosure of a social injustice expressed by a mother and daughter. Yes, she was disturbed by the injustice of the rapes both women had experienced, but it was her response in the session to the women's disclosures that disturbed her the most! She had gasped, covered her mouth, and said, "Oh, no, how terrible!" But the mother and daughter stood, reached out to each other and for several moments held one another in a long supportive hug. She (the new family therapist) felt hot tears burning her eyes as she sat silently and humbly witnessed the healing taking place in the room.

She didn't recall what she said next but it didn't really matter as questions about her "Oh no" and her tears were dominating her thinking. She was questioning her response and feeling embarrassed and ashamed that she had let her reactions to the injustices experienced by the women be so transparent. "I really need to learn to contain my reactions and emotions," she stated in a small, uncertain voice.

I quietly asked, "What would it mean to you if you could bear witness to the accounts of people who have experienced traumatic injustices and not feel anything or experience any kind of visceral reaction?" "It would mean their experiences were not important and that I was prepared to turn away from the injustices they experienced!" Her voice grew stronger and within moments she was sitting tall. Our conversation soon ended but not before the therapist stated a new commitment to pursuing her understanding of how to do social justice talk in family therapy. And she did.

Transformative practice occurs on many different fronts. In this story, the therapist's ability to create an opportunity for a mother and daughter to talk about their traumatic experiences in healing ways disrupted the injustices of the shame-filled silence that had previously enshrouded their relationship. Their courage and that of the therapist transformed isolation and shame into unity and hope. The therapeutic process also created an opportunity for the women to make sense of each other's behaviors in more respectful ways. This process led to the women deciding to work on developing mutual support for one another among a large, complex family system. The family later shared with the therapist that the daughter had begun to interact differently with her boyfriend and some of her friends at school, which they saw as evidence that the changes being made within the family were important to the daughter and would have results beyond their family system.

Transformational practice also occurred during the impromptu supervision session. The idea that "therapists need to be objective and emotionally contained beings" was disrupted and an opportunity for alternative perspectives on how to handle one's reactions during a difficult session was opened up. As the therapist and supervisor engaged in an exploration of the meanings connected to various optional responses, the therapist's commitment to learning how to engage in social justice talk was strengthened.

But the transformation process did not end there. Recently, I received an email from a former family therapy intern who has an ongoing contact with the therapist mentioned in the above account. She shared that a group of therapists, including the therapist mentioned above, are meeting to support one another as they continue to work in ways that address social injustices in family therapy. This news was encouraging to me and I trust this account will encourage others to continue to engage in transformational practices.

- *Do we have a right to thoughtfully consider our sense of outrage as we hear client stories of mistreatment?*
- *Can we seriously examine how we, as therapists, might be implicated in promoting and/or perpetuating injustices with our clients?*
- *When might/does/could our sense of outrage or devastation become unhelpful to our clients? And maybe even oppressive to our clients?*
- *How could we make the case that attending to issues of social justice is not our job—either as a front line therapist, supervisor, researcher, or teacher?*
- *How might we determine if showing strong emotions over mistreatment or injustice with a client is useful to them? Is there a way we could inquire about this directly with our clients?*

Reflections: the Ups and Downs of Transformative Experiences

By Faye

Faye brings forward that personal transformations can be a mixed blessing—they can carry change and goodness, and they can also carry along with them change and sorrow. As much as we promote and work for transformative practices, holding a justice perspective would have us remember that even changes made with the best of intentions can have "fallout" and we are well advised to recognize that change and transformation can come with a cost too. As therapists, we oftentimes oversell the advantages of change without respectfully acknowledging the difficulties that may also be a part of the process.

As an intern at the Calgary Family Therapy Centre (CFTC), I feel like I experienced exponential growth in my understanding of what social justice is and what it looks like in practice. And yet, I feel like the blindfolded individual who just discovered the ear of the proverbial elephant.

Previous to my training, I had experienced social justice mainly as a catch phrase. One that I was deeply interested in learning how to apply; sure, but it was nonetheless a phrase that carried that aspirational quality we find in our codes of ethics, along with little guidance for how to translate those great aspirations into meaningful change in the day-to-day moments of actual lived experience. I will reflect on my process of learning in this regard.

I began my Master's degree at an institution (Athabasca University) that provides distributed learning; most courses are carried out online, while a small number involve face-to-face training. Aware that there is a cultural bias (particularly in PhD programs) against online learning, I made this choice because at the outset, I was a stay-at-home mother who lived in rural Nova Scotia, and this was the best, if not only, fit for me. However, when it came time to find a practicum placement, there were none to be found locally.

I applied to the CFTC, and moved across the country to train with a group of dedicated professionals who carry strong values of openness and inclusion. The commonality among the various professionals who have been involved in my training, either as clinical supervisors at CFTC or as faculty at Athabasca University, is their openness and responsiveness to me as a learner, and their facility in opening doors to enhance my learning and professional development.

This "facility" has at times involved the usual things, such as creating space for interested students to participate in their work, perhaps by helping them with literature reviews, or presenting at conferences with them, or on their behalf. My mentors have gone beyond this, however, as I have experienced opportunities to participate directly in their research (see Snyder, McIntosh, and Gosnell, Learning to Speak Social Justice Talk in Family Therapy, 2015); to work alongside them as a teaching assistant; and to observe their own colleagues from around Canada and the world whom they have hosted in an effort to create opportunities for interns to see how other family therapists work.

As such, my process of learning has been very iterative and multifaceted. It has involved a lot of movement between theory and practice, and classroom and clinic. The research meetings at the CFTC, however, were particularly poignant foci for integrating and operationalizing knowledge about seemingly abstract concepts and ethical ideals. These meetings were specifically geared at addressing issues of social-justice-in-practice with an interdisciplinary group, in a reflexive manner, which added a significant boost to the overall learning environment. In terms of process, I would say this was one of the richest forums for enhancing learning.

The question of how to transform the overarching system we call "culture" for the greater benefit of all still remains elusive for me, but less so. I have come to see how discourses and practices reflect one another, and that transforming the broader context can indeed happen through seemingly minor acts, including (sometimes especially) conversational acts. My training has created many opportunities to contemplate on-the-ground possibilities for systemic change and to formulate questions of increasing complexity that drive deeper and deeper into the heart of this issue.

While I have experienced immeasurable personal and professional growth, my time in Calgary did not come without significant personal cost. My partner and daughter were unable to come with me, as he owns a business back in Nova Scotia that he was not able to leave. Our relationship did not survive the physical separation, and our once-intact family is now in limbo with respect to who should live where, as I continue to work toward the licensing requirements of the profession of psychology, which vary across Canadian jurisdictions. Despite these challenges, I remain grateful for the learning opportunities, and hopefully I will be able to carry forward and share with others what I have learned about transformative practice.

I wish to acknowledge and thank Drs. Karl Tomm, Lynda Snyder, Sally St. George, Dan Wulff, Joanne Schulz-Hall, Jeff Chang, Paul Jerry, and Emily Doyle for being generous, committed, and exemplary counseling professionals. There would be no transformative practice for novices if the opportunities to learn the "how" of it were not opened and facilitated by those like you.

- *How, as clinicians, do we to stay humble and curious regarding a topic like social justice?*
- *Do we notice the differences in social injustices that people face by factoring in their relative positions of location and privilege? (In other words, social injustice may better be thought of as plural.)*
- *What are the relative advantages and disadvantages of thinking of social justice as a process versus a goal?*
- *Is it possible for a person to accept certain social injustices that they are facing rather than work to change them? Do they have the right to decide this for themselves?*
- *If a therapist sees a situation in therapy as an example of a social injustice and the client does not, how might this difference be handled?*

The Transformation from Heartbreak

By Lynda A.

Most of us who work in this helping field live privileged lives. Or as the lyrics from a song from the musical, Aida, *say, "We live extravagant lives." That does not mean that we get only to witness injustices happening to others on our caseloads or in our clinics or that we are immune from experiencing them directly. They hurt us too, and we can learn from them. Lynda A. takes us into one such moment.*

There was a young boy, about 7 years old, who learned a lot by listening to and imagining what grownups meant when they said stuff with hushed and serious voices. He carefully watched their faces and he protected himself from the hard things they were saying by running into the other room or getting mad and hitting his brother and distracting everyone. He didn't really want to listen to what they were saying, because it wasn't really a thing that a boy wants to imagine—that his mom could get really sick and die. So he continued doing the stuff that kids do—he went to school where he really wanted to learn to read, but where he also learned that the letters could shape-shift before his eyes, making it really hard to follow the words. He didn't like sitting still, and he loved to imagine he was a detective figuring out mysteries—or a Jedi knight fighting "bad guys." You yourselves, who were once 7 years old, can imagine the challenges in this boy's life.

The people who cared about this boy wanted to help him learn to read because he loved books so much. And even though there were lots of other things going on in this family, they took him to see a psychologist to get some answers about why the letters kept flopping around on the page when the boy looked at them. The psychologist spent a lot of time, and many visits, asking the boy to answer questions. To make it entertaining for himself, the boy sometimes would make up answers different from what he thought the psychologist wanted to hear. And sometimes he would refuse to answer, or hold out for a candy, or ask to go the bathroom again. His mom, who was still dying, would sit in the waiting room and patiently take him to the bathroom or coax him back into the "testing room." The psychologist saw the effects of the chemo, and the declining health of the mom, but beyond asking about her diagnosis in the first meeting didn't think that it was relevant to how the boy was doing in school.

The story takes lots of twists and turns from beginning to end, but one place to end is with the psychologist's report that was produced for the boy's school and which was read by the teachers a few weeks after the mom died. In that 32-page report with lots of words that could flip themselves around and fall off the pages, there was a single sentence that indicated that the mom had cancer—it was on page 2. There was no reference to the influence of the illness or anticipated death of his mother in the recommendations for how the teachers might support his learning and behavior in class. The boy has caring teachers, aunts, uncles, grandparents, cousins, lots of friends, and a great brother and dad. His imagination and these people who love him and care for his well-being, along with his warm home, clothes, and food, will support him as he overcomes lots of obstacles in his life. But the part of the story that I, as one of his aunts, struggle with is that a well-intentioned professional totally ignored the context of this boy's troubles.

I'm not feeling that creative and generative in my work right now—because I'm still grieving the loss of my sister—that's to be expected and I know that. But I am motivated and driven by this front-row seat I had for a year in the life of my nephew. Context is important—in fact, my current experience tells me that it is pretty much "everything." I now take greater care as a teacher and supervisor to describe our profession to new students as "systemic and relational therapy," and to talk about what that means. These probably weren't ever just words to me, but they have taken on new prominence in my understanding of our work. We pay particular attention to the broader systemic and structural influences on people's lives and to the ever-present influences of their primary relationships. If this boy lived in a family that was marginalized, isolated, or poor or in a neighborhood or home where there was an ongoing threat of violence, his life would be even more difficult. As a therapist (and supervisor and researcher), I can't afford to *not* ask the necessary questions about systems, structures, and relationships. The people who come to me for assistance can't afford for me to fail to support them in resisting the messages that lead them to blame themselves for social injustice. The work we do matters in the lives of the people with whom we work. Training new professionals to ask the systemic, structural, and relational questions, and to take these responses into account in understanding context, also matters. Mentoring new researchers to look to relational interactions, broader context, and social justice issues in examining contemporary family life is work that matters. Maintaining an awareness of our own context—the gifts of insight and experience, the challenges of blinders and narrow perspectives—also matter.

- *What are the consequences of simplifying or "cleaning" complexity?*
- *With an appreciation of the complexity of context, how much should we take into consideration?*
- *How do we sort through the intersections of our contexts and those of our clients? When do these intersections open space for growth and change? When do these intersections blind us or restrain us?*
- *What limitations do our disciplinary trainings impose on our conceptualizing? How can we address these limitations and still work within our chosen disciplines?*
- *When our disciplinary stances conflict with other professionals' disciplinary stances, how can we navigate these differences without personalizing the struggle?*

Our Part in the System: A Social Justice in Family Therapy Story

By Shannon

Claiming a social justice stance is relatively easy. But can we see our own role in the messes we usually attribute to the systems in which we operate? Shannon recounts her renewed attention to the structural fences our own professions build. She highlights the thorny problem of multiple service coordination and the burden placed on service users to find ways to articulate a variety of services that are not designed to work in a coordinated fashion.

During my initial meeting with the V Family, Darlene (the mother) shared with me that she suffers from Post-Traumatic Stress Disorder. Not until the third session with this family did I learn that this mental illness developed as a result of child abuse and had been triggered due to her family members' recent ICU hospital admissions from traumatic events. Hence, in working with the V Family and recognizing their experience with trauma, I aimed to be vigilant in ensuring that power was in their hands in terms of what they choose to share and what interventions they chose to take up.

I also recognized that Darlene's story was characterized by chronic feelings of isolation and disconnection. Her ongoing struggles with depressive symptoms, verbal aggression, and addictive behavior seemed to be shaped by the complex intersection of personal experiences and the social structures, institutions, class, and gender. As a result of her experience, the family appeared to be affected by her trauma and she seemed to be influenced by theirs.

Though Darlene has actively taken the initiative to seek help for her mental health concerns, she shared with me that she has experienced difficulty navigating a fragmented mental health system that often fails to focus on the needs of the family as a *whole*. During our therapy sessions, Darlene also shared that the mental health services she has been able to access center their approaches on behavior modification and medication compliance—methods that she has not found helpful. These approaches seem to reinforce a belief that mental health is an individual problem and that changes can only occur due to the efforts, decisions, and behavior of the mentally ill person.

In addition to Darlene's own mental health struggles, she was concerned that one of her children was developing similar concerns. Darlene's worries brought me to think about the way in which anxiety can present as a pattern in families and that the environmental influences appear to represent the greatest contribution to the intergenerational transmission of fear. These expressed feelings also impressed on me the notion that mental illness is not only felt by the individual, but the family as a whole, particularly children.

Although the impact of parental mental illness and the development of children have been studied for many years, available treatment services for adults, parents, and their families have been fragmented due to the mental health system's categorical approach to service delivery. Despite the evidence that supports the need for more family-focused collaborative and integrated child and adult mental health services, these services continue to be disjointed which seems to take away from the focus on family needs.

In my developing role as a family therapist, I feel I have an ethical and moral responsibility to recognize social injustice issues such as the oppression that can be experienced within the health care system. Recognizing and challenging the ways in which societal patterns of domination are woven into the fabric of family life has been a highlight in my clinical social work learning and I hope to continue to play a part in dismantling these oppressive societal discourses.

Identifying and meeting a family's needs, helping to navigate the system, and expanding choices and opportunities are a few of the ways I feel I can uphold social justice principles. Through incorporating social justice talk into therapeutic conversations, clinical social workers can contribute to enhanced family harmony as well as a more socially just world.

- *What is our responsibility to address the discoordination of the helping systems within which we work?*
- *How might we respond to our agencies/institutions when client service is hampered or compromised by economic considerations for the maintenance of the agency/institution?*
- *Is it reasonable to locate behaviors at either pole of a fair–unfair, just–unjust continuum or are they more appropriately located somewhere in the middle?*

Community-based Participatory Practice—Research of a Different Kind

By Ron

Ron demonstrates an example of taking the practices he and his colleagues have developed to new levels by meaningfully including the clients/patients in practice and clinical research. This softening of the distinction between professionals and clients opens new possibilities for learning and development, while simultaneously validating those persons who have been traditionally only "acted upon." Having students offering fresh thinking to teams is a way of conceptualizing that generates more hope and value than viewing students as simply low in a hierarchy and in need of training.

For the past couple of years, I have been working with a team of researchers from Penn State University College of Medicine, the University of Nebraska-Lincoln, and Loyola University Maryland focusing on ways we can help improve and enhance the role patients play in the development and application of clinical research in clinical practice and ultimately in the lives of patients and their families. We have worked closely with the Patient-Centered Outcome Research Institute (PCORI; http://www.pcori.org/) to learn from previously published qualitative and mixed-method research accounts as to how patients, family members, and primary care physicians have given their voices to inform research design and results translation and to discover new insights from these stakeholders via interviews and qualitative data analysis in our own research.

To carry out this work, we employ a design approach called "Community-Based Participatory Research" (Minkler and Wallerstein 2008) wherein we, as principal investigators, "soften" the traditional categories between researcher and participant so we recruit patients, family members, and physicians to become part of the research leadership team. They then become decision-makers with us throughout the research process participating in all aspects of conceptualization, implementation, dissemination, and evaluation. As a result, we all not only learn new knowledge, but also new ways of practicing clinical research and providing care.

When I was writing *Everyday Solution-Focused Recursion: When Family Therapy Faculty, Supervisors, Researchers, Students, and Clients Play Well Together* (Chenail et al. 2016) with my colleagues at Nova Southeastern University,

I came to realize our work could also be seen as community-based participatory research or maybe more accurately, community-based participatory *practice*. We have softened our traditional teacher–student, therapist–patient, and researcher–participant roles to appreciate what others can contribute to making our community and the lives of the people who live in it better. We actively recruit clients to help us redesign our clinical practice, research participants to enhance our research practice, and students to help us learn new practices. In the process, they all learn new practices too.

As I read the other chapters in this book, I became inspired to transform the two qualitative research courses I teach in our PhD in Family Therapy program. To do so I have been imagining how I can embrace the notions of daily practices and social justice more fully in how I approach the classes. To start the process, I have been using a community-based participatory research design reaching out to former students from a continuum of those still taking classes in the PhD program, those in the dissertation process, and those who have completed the dissertation and graduated from the program. In my outreach efforts, I am asking three open-ended questions: "What should I continue doing, what should I stop doing, and what should I start doing?" I am also asking the same questions of my fellow faculty members who, too, work with PhD students on their dissertations. Lastly, I will ask the PhD students who will be taking these courses in 2016, "What they should continue doing, stop doing, and start doing in order to successfully complete their PhDs?" In addition, I will share with them the ideas presented in this book and encourage them to begin softening their categories, embracing new daily practices, and transforming their learning class-by-class.

I am not really sure what will come from this community-based participatory effort. Will the classes stay the same? Will there be a complete overhaul? Am I even the right person to teach these classes? I know change can be good and it also can be scary. Yet, I remain hopeful in the collective wisdom of our community and believe they will offer some wonderful insight and suggestions. I also hope this outreach will have a further transformative influence on our department and college. Finally, if I have learned anything at all from this book it is that social transformative practice starts with oneself—so let the daily practice begin one personal, transformative moment at a time.

- *If we softened the distinctions between therapist and client, researcher and participant, supervisor and supervisee, and teacher and student, what possibilities would be available?*
- *In softening these professional and disciplinary distinctions, what drawbacks could we imagine?*
- *What specific benefits accrue to the therapist, researcher, supervisor, and teacher to reformulate their relationships with clients, participants, supervisees, and students?*
- *How many of these professional relationships can be adjusted within the current structures of therapy and academia? Do the larger structures within which we work need to be modified or reformulated?*

A Corporate Apology?

By Dan

Dan tells a story of observing a recent family session. He demonstrates that even with decades of experience, there is room for new learning and seeing what was previously unseen and unheard and the difference that can make in understanding change and transformation. Being open to seeing and hearing new ideas in how to work with families is itself a challenge, particularly when one has developed comfortable and well-worn assumptions.

Recently, I observed a family therapy session in which a father and 15-year-old son were in entrenched disagreement with many derogatory statements being made back-and-forth. In family therapy, these sorts of pained interactions are not unusual. But the frame drawn around this family's trouble by the therapist and team made this session very out of the ordinary for me. The conversation in the room and the therapist's discussion with the team behind the mirror led to a strikingly different conceptualization of this family and the distress they were living out, one that brought an aspect of the family's life that is typically considered "external" and possibly historical to a position that was front-and-center.

The rift between the father and the son began in earnest 5 years prior when the father was laid-off from a professional position that he had held for 15 years (the father was the primary breadwinner for this family). This led to a period of unemployment before the father landed another job in a city far away from the city where they had been living for 15 years. This necessitated an uprooting of the boy from his school and friends that he had developed over his entire life. The son was very upset about the move and voiced the unfairness of it from his point of view. The new job turned out to be short-lived as the father was again laid-off due to corporate downsizing. This led to another family move that was again tumultuous for the whole family and in particular, the son. The arguing and fighting continued as the son blamed his father for the moves and all the turmoil the boy was feeling. The stress the parents were experiencing was not understood by the boy. They were under extreme stress due to the forced moves too, but the bickering that escalated between the boy and his dad became "personal" and they each blamed the other for their fouled relationship and the blaming of the other begat defensive responses.

For me, the punctuation of the family troubles as beginning and fueled by the unanticipated and forced relocations for the father's employment that were discussed in the therapy session and in the therapy team conversations opened my eyes to role of the corporations in this family's stress. The in-fighting the family was experiencing highlighted for me the role of employers (corporations) in the life of this family. On the constructive side, the income provided by the employer is the primary element that supports the family in its lifestyle. On the flip side, the withdrawal of that income casts the family adrift in an effort to re-establish its economic footing. The role of finance in the well-being of family life is well-known, but what is less acknowledged is the role of financial withdrawal in encouraging and exacerbating interpersonal troubles. We tend to accept the idea that corporate decisions trump family life.

The team behind the mirror posed the question: "Why don't employers/corporations acknowledge/apologize to families for the harm caused by their market-driven decisions?" Initially this seemed like a nonsensical question but then I asked myself, "why not pose this question?" Too often, we automatically dismiss/condone what larger systems do to families and in therapy; we tend to act in ways that support the notion that families are the sole architects of their troubles (and therefore the location for remediation of those troubles). I am now seeing this traditional mental health approach as an illusion and mystification that in effect permits larger systems to be unaccountable for their actions on its employees. As a family therapist, this family therapy session reminded me of how easy it is for us as therapists to narrow our conceptual lenses to only see the aftermath of injustices and then converse with families in ways suggestive that they, and they alone, are responsible for the troubles they face and the changes they must make.

- *What is an "external event or circumstance" in the life of a family?*
- *What are the consequences of misattributing responsibility?*
- *What would an apology from an employer to a family look like? Is an apology enough in this instance, or would an expectation of change in how the employer "does business" be necessary to legitimize the apology?*
- *What other "external" events/circumstances have the potential to disrupt a family's interactions and avoid our therapeutic scrutiny?*
- *Is it possible to trace back* all *family conflict to external events/circumstances that pushed them into untenable situations which then spawned intra-family conflict? Could it be that family conflict/violence is the consequence or symptom of injustice?*

Closing

In reading over this chapter of stories, Ron offers a new challenge to each of us. He said,

> As I read the other authors' transformational accounts in this chapter along with my own piece, I was struck by the series of binary or dyadic distinctions we drew in our transformative conversations: justice/injustice, internal/external, treatment/mistreatment, novice/expert, therapist/client, teacher/student, and transformative/sameness. This made me wonder: What if we put on our triadic and systemic lenses? What would we start to see if we looked for relational patterns among more than two points? In my instance, what would my research class look like if I softened all the categories among teacher/student/researcher/participant/therapist/client? I am not sure, but I am excited to see where a triadic-plus transformational view takes me.

We, Dan and Sally, agree that maybe part of our difficulty in articulating the experience of transformational change in addressing social justice issues is being committed to our language of binaries. It seems very out-of-character for us to espouse a systemic view that embraces complexity while still so easily languaging events and experiences in the world as "either this or that." Using binaries/dichotomies may be our efforts to better manage our complex and ever-changing world, but at the cost of over-simplifying it and rendering our efforts at change as thin or superficial. We need to take the advice we offer each other, our colleagues, and students when confronted with an either/or framing. We ask, what is a third or fourth way that could be used to think about this? We deliberately use the language of third and fourth ways to avoid dichotomizing binaries with complexities (demonizing binaries and valorizing complexities)—each idea explored is worthy. We just want to emphasize that we should question the confidence we hold when options are displayed as either this or that.

Reference

Minkler, M., & Wallerstein, N. (Eds.). (2008). *Community-based participatory research for health: From process to outcomes* (2nd ed.). San Francisco, CA: Jossey-Bass.

Index

A
Addressing, 4, 5, 19, 48, 89, 97
Analysis and Synthesis, 62
Agents of change, 65
Appraising, 34, 35
Appreciative andragogy, 70
"As if", 18
Assumptions, 4, 10, 12, 27, 29, 32, 35, 43, 45, 46, 52, 66, 70, 81, 96
Attending and reflecting, 52

B
Binaries, 97, 98
Boundaries, 69, 70, 74, 78–80
Brief therapy Institute, 73, 76, 79

C
Calgary family therapy centre (CFTC), 57, 89
Clinical social work, 58, 59
Co-create, 70–72, 76, 79, 82
Collaborative/collective action, 65
Co-measure, 71, 72, 82
Community-based participatory practice, 94, 95
Community-minded family therapy, 5
Community therapy, 20
Complexity, 51, 90, 92, 98
Conception of
  Initial engagement, 60
  study, 60
Confidentiality, 14, 16
Consciousness-raising, 66
Context, 5, 10, 12, 15, 16–18, 28, 34, 41–43, 45–48, 53, 54, 63, 64, 75, 90–92
Cooperative Inquiry, 60
Counseling psychology, 58

D
Daily practice, research as, 25, 29, 31–33
Daily practices, 6, 95
Diagnosis, 47, 91
Dichotomies, 98
Dyadic, 42, 45, 97

E
Education, 1, 2
Effective consumers of research, 33
Emotions, 67, 87, 88
Engaging generative dialogue, 43
Entitlement, 86
Ethical imperative, 60
Extra-familial, 9, 10, 13

F
Family dynamics, 2
Family therapy
  intern, 88
  practices, 85
  program, 95
  session, 96, 97
  stories, 85
Finances, 96
Foundational skills, 43–45

G
Generative conversations, 43, 44, 65
Gestation Period, the, 61

H
Hardening of the categories, 69, 79
Healing interpersonal patterns (HIPs), 31
Hierarchy, 70, 79
Hope, 72, 78, 80

S. St. George and D. Wulff (eds.), *Family Therapy as Socially Transformative Practice*, AFTA SpringerBriefs in Family Therapy,
DOI 10.1007/978-3-319-29188-8

I
Individualism, 2
Inside/outside therapy, 15
Insoo Kim Berg, 75–77, 80
Integrate, 10, 17
Integrating, 26, 27
Internal dialogue, 63
Internal/external, 97
Intersectionalities, 62
Intervention, Research as, 27
Intra-family, 9, 19
Inviting and utilizing, 45
Isolation, 16, 20

J
Just therapy, 19
Just/unjust, 14

L
Language/languaging, 1, 2, 16, 21, 97
Larger systems, 14
Lead from behind, 71
Learning to speak, 57
Learnings about learning, 62

M
Macro/micro, 11, 17
Marriage and family therapy, 10, 17
Mapping, 25, 45, 54
Meaning-making, 57, 58
Micro-practices, 59, 62, 64
Miracle question, 75, 78, 80
Modelling, 65
Multiple perspectives, 45

N
Novice therapists, 41, 43, 44, 46, 47

O
Operationalize, 61
Outside/inside therapy, 14, 15

P
Pathologizing interpersonal patterns (PIPs), 31, 32
Personal transformation, 88
PIPs/HIPs, 31
Power, 6, 22, 28, 43, 46–49, 51, 52, 54, 62, 64, 7, 78, 93
Powerlessness, 47–49
Practice-based evidence, 25, 29
Practitioner-based inquiry, 57
Practitioner, Researcher as, 25
Professional stance, 87

R
Recursion, 6, 70–72, 81, 82, 94
Reflecting on shifting, 46
Reflecting on various dimensions position, 46
Reflecting on various dimensions power, 46
Reflecting team, 61, 63, 64
Reflection(s), 61–65
Reflective practices, 62
Reflexive practices, 62–65
Reflexivity, 65
Relational, 1, 6, 91, 92, 97
Research, 1, 2, 5, 6, 72–74, 77, 78, 80, 82, 89, 94
Research As Daily Practice, 19, 57, 60
Research plans
  clarifying, 61
  collaborating, 61
Researcher, 5, 92, 94
Researcher, Practitioner as, 25
Researching clinicians, 72, 73
Researching practitioner, the, 5, 27

S
Scaling, 82
Screening(s), 57, 61
Self-awareness, 43, 49, 50, 52
Service coordination, 92
Social action, 66
Social change, 65, 66
Social constructionism, 1, 57
Social injustice, 58, 60, 63, 66
Social Justice
  concepts, 59
  conversations, 62, 63, 65
  practicalities, 59
  talk, 57, 59–62, 64–67
Social location and intersections, 52
Socially transformative practice, 59, 65–67
Social systems, 59, 62, 66
Social work, 1, 2, 10, 16, 17, 93
Societal discourses, 1, 5, 6, 9, 12–14, 93
Soften the categories, 72, 81
Solution-focused, 6, 69–75, 77–79, 81, 82, 95
Solution-focused brief therapy (SFBT), 70, 73, 75, 76, 80, 81
Stories, 6, 15, 16, 32, 47, 52, 72, 80, 85–88, 97
Strengths, 70–72, 79

Stretching customary, 85
Supervision/Supervisor, 1, 5, 6, 73–76, 78, 81, 88, 89, 91
Supporting development, 41
Systems, 2, 85, 92, 97

T
Teaching, 27, 29, 32–35, 73, 77, 79, 82
Teaching clinicians, 33
Therapeutic conversations, 59, 60, 64, 65
Therapeutic injustice, 58
Therapeutic practice, 63
Therapist self-awareness, 49
Therapy room, 43
Transdisciplinary, 17
Transformational learning, 66
Transformative, 71–74, 81
Transformative experiences
  downs, 88
  ups, 88
Transformative/transformational respect, 59, 65–67
Transforming practices, 6, 95
Trauma, 44, 45, 93

V
Venn diagram, 26
Vulnerability, 60, 66, 67

CPSIA information can be obtained
at www.ICGtesting.com
Printed in the USA
LVHW021732090523
746516LV00004B/260

9 783319 291864